MW00874523

Rebel Pulpit

The Civil War Prison Diary of Lt. James Vance Walker
Company G – Third Tennessee Confederate Infantry

Joe Walker

"For which I am suffering even to the point of being chained like a criminal. But God's word is not chained."
2 Timothy 2:9

Rebel Pulpit: The Civil War Prison Diary of Lt. James Vance Walker – Company G – Third Tennessee Confederate Infantry

All bible references are from the King James Version of the Holy Bible.

For more information on obtaining additional copies of this book or to contact the author, visit www.1864arkansas.com

For
Gracie

Acknowledgements

When my cousin, Mary Guthrie, sent me a copy of James Vance Walker's diary several years ago, I knew immediately it had to be published so others could enjoy it. Mary and I share a love of genealogy and she has, over the years, shared much information with me about my Tennessee Walker family, filling in several gaps in my research. If there is anyone who deserves credit for "Rebel Pulpit," it is Mary Guthrie, for whom I am forever grateful.

Equally, someone who I discovered during my research who has fast become a friend is Laura Lee, the Interpretive Program Manager and Park Historian at Fort Delaware State Park. Laura opened doors for me during my research enabling me to obtain additional research material that significantly improved "Rebel Pulpit."

J. Branden Mackie of the Fort Delaware Society, a group dedicated to preserving the story of Fort Delaware, was invaluable in providing some of the photographs you see in the book, especially those of Reverend Handy.

Don Handy, who provided me with research material on his ancestor, Reverend Isaac W.K. Handy. Having Reverend Handy's diary accompanying James Vance Walker's diary only enhances the story.

To my editor, Melissa Hadley. Over the last five years, Melissa has listened to my ideas, stood by me when I've become frustrated and lost focus. She has been my compass, forever pulling me back on track toward the goal. She is more than my editor and much more than my friend. She is an amazing inspiration. Future generations will owe her forever for helping to bring these stories to life.

To my wife, Allie. Once again, you've indulged me as I've taken a walk into history to preserve a story for future generations. You've listened for what seems like a thousand hours as I've read – and reread – and reread – sections of my book to you, all the while encouraging me to keep moving on those days I would get discouraged. To say I love you would be an understatement.

To my children, Lauren Elizabeth and Stephen Ryan. My hope is that I am leaving a trail behind with these books that one day you will follow and carry on. As I write this, Lauren received the 8th grade outstanding history student award – well done! Stephen Ryan is still a bit too little to grasp all of this history stuff, but I'm confident he will one day walk in my shoes in my love of history.

And lastly and certainly not least is my friend Cindi Smith. Cindi was the very first to purchase my first book, "Harvest of Death: The Battle of Jenkins' Ferry, Arkansas" and has made a commitment to be the first to purchase any future book I write. If that's not friendship, I don't know what is.

Introduction

This is not a diary in a conventional sense, but rather a recollection of the efforts of a group of Confederate soldiers confined in a Federal Prison during the Civil War to create a religious presence within the prison during the incarceration.

These men seemed driven to establish some sense of order, of normalcy, in the midst of chaos. Just as organized religion today seeks to create bonds of stability in an unstable world, so these soldiers sought to be the same 150 years ago.

Prior to his capture by Federal soldiers in February 1864, James Vance Walker had served as First Lieutenant commanding Company "G" of the Third Tennessee Confederate Infantry (Vaughn's Brigade). He was my great-great uncle. His father, William Houston Walker, my great-great grandfather, also served as a private in the Third Tennessee for the duration of the war.

The Civil War tore my Walker family literally apart. James Vance's uncle, Daniel Walker, sided with the Union Army, enlisting in the Third Tennessee Union Cavalry. Captured in 1864, Daniel Walker was incarcerated in the Confederate POW prison in Cahaba, Alabama. Released at the end of the war, Daniel Walker, along with scores of recently released prisoners, were placed aboard the steamer "Sultana' which exploded near Memphis on April 26, 1865. Daniel Walker's body was never recovered. At the conclusion of the Civil War, the pro-Union members of the Walker family migrated westward, settling in southern Illinois, leaving James Vance Walker and the pro-Southern members of the family behind.

In a 1914 Civil War veteran's questionnaire, James Vance Walker referred to himself as "a poor Christian." After the war, he would serve as a Deacon in his local Church in McMinn County, Tennessee. His religious activities before the war are unknown due to the lack of biographical information. It is his Civil War diary where his religious fervor is clearly revealed.

Throughout the diary, Walker mentioned the Reverend Isaac W.K. Handy, a Virginia minister imprisoned at Fort Delaware prison as a political prisoner. Reverend Handy maintained an extensive daily written log during his incarceration. He published his diary in 1874. In order to enhance the significance of Walker's diary, I have included segments of Reverend Handy's diary that corresponds to specific dates mentioned in Walker's diary.

There are extensive footnotes to identify specific events and occurrences that the diary mentions. There is also an attempt, through the footnotes to identify as many of the men mentioned in the diary as possible. I regret not all could be identified. The diary offers the reader a glimpse into the efforts of men, so long ago, who sought to save men's souls.

Table of Contents

James Vance Walker

The Diary

U.S. Military Prison Officers Barracks

Fort Delaware, Delaware

We design in the proceeding sketches to show as familiar as possible the rise and progress of the religious element in our midst during the first three months of our confinement on this island. And the gradual development of those Christian graces that ought always to characterize the desciples [sic] of our Lord and master. We feel a deep sense of our inability to do justice to a subject so very important. So let these few preliminary remarks suffice.

And we will begin back at the time of our departure from Camp Chase, Ohio.

On Friday, March 25th 1864 two hundred and seventy two Confederate officers held as prisoners of war at Camp Chase[1] Ohio

---

[1] Camp Chase military prison, located in present day Columbus, Ohio, was established in May 1861, becoming one of the five largest Confederate prison camps in the north. Named for Salmon P. Chase, former Governor of Ohio and later serving as Secretary of Treasury under President Abraham Lincoln, the prison would at its peak hold over 10,000 Confederate soldiers. The camp cemetery holds the remains of over 2,000 Confederate soldiers who died while incarcerated at Camp Chase. The camp was closed at the end of the Civil War with the land being sold in the 1930's for private development.

left that post heavily guarded by the 88[2]th Ohio Regiment. They were marched to the depot at Columbus where transportation awaited them to this island. At the railroad station they were joined by the sixty nine officers from Brigadier General John H. Morgan's[3] cavalry command who had suffered a long and painful incarceration in the Ohio state prison. Soon they were on their journey hither. Buoyant with the hope that they were homeward bound and would soon reach the will of their own beloved country. So manfully struggling to drive an unrelenting fore from her borders. We were so closely guarded that we could only catch an occasional glimpse of the Yankee land as we passed along. About 2 O'Clock p.m. on Sunday march 27th [1864] we arrived at Philadelphia where an immense multitude of the curious had assembled to see those who had endured so much for their bleeding country. We were marched on board the steamer Oscola and as our vessel moved off into the Delaware river, defening [sic] cheers were raised for the land of Dixie while the gazing multitude were left on the shore. We arrived

---

[2] The 88th Ohio Infantry Regiment was organized at Camp Chase, near Columbus, Ohio in July 1862, serving the majority of the war on guard duty at Camp Chase. The regiment was mustered out of service at Camp Chase on July 3, 1865.

[3] John Hunt Morgan (1825-1864) was a Confederate Brigadier General, known for his raid ("Morgan's Raid") in the summer of 1863 where Morgan led his Confederate Cavalry over 1,000 miles from Tennessee to Kentucky through Indiana into Southern Ohio. This was the farthest point north reached by any Confederate unit.

at this post about 8 o'clock p.m. and occupied quarters previously prepared for us.[4]

---

[4] **Handy Diary: Monday, March 28, 1864:** We had an unusual excitement, this morning, caused by the arrival of three hundred and thirty-three Confederate officers, some sixty of whom belong to Morgan's command, and directly from the Ohio Penitentiary. The others are from Camp Chase. Among the number are Gen. Vance, of North Carolina, and Col. Dick, and Capt. Charlton Morgan, brothers of the General. The inmates of [barracks] No. 1 were ordered to vacate their room immediately and to occupy [barracks] No. 3, the object being the accommodation of certain superior officers. A general disorder ensued – the discomfited movers complaining on account of their loss by the exchange – [barracks] No. 3 being a side room, and considerably smaller than the one to be left. The white-washers and scourers were soon at work, and the vacated room was ready in double-quick time. It was late, however, before [barracks] No. 3 could be in order. Difficulties arose about a stove, which led to unpleasant words with [barracks] No. 4, and which was after awhile settled by an exchange of stoves between [barracks] No. 1 and [barracks] No. 3. Four officers, at length, made their appearance, and took possession of their quarters, with a wet floor. Three of the new-comers are Captains, and one a Lieutenant. Their names are Cunningham, Coombs, Croxton and Taylor. Civilities were offered by the old occupants of the prison; but the strangers informed us that they were under parole not to communicate with us, and as they seemed shy, and reserved, they were shortly left to themselves, and their own reflection. Col. Drake coming up in the afternoon, stated that the four strangers were all Kentuckians, and that they were preparing to "galvanize." The pleasure anticipated from their accession was not realized, and little has since been heard or seen of the party.

My wife has returned from Baltimore, having failed to secure a personal interview with the "Commission," but not without considerable information from Col. Purnell, who communicated with the Judges, and reported to her accordingly. She learns that the man who informed against me was Snyder, and that he endeavored to make the most unfavorable impression, by representing me as the most violent man in the prison; and that I had been a regular mail agent for the South, and had shown Shanks the way to run the blockade. My wife, also, states that through some strange misapprehension, the Judges had gotten the impression that I am now willing to take the oak of allegiance. Perhaps the technical, and literal response to their late letter of

18

The first few weeks at Fort Delaware is indeed a sad picture to be drawn. The occurences [sic] of that time are not such as should appear on these pages except so far as may be necessary to show the moral conditions of our fellow prisoners at that time. Intoxicating liquors were sold by the Sutler[5] and their use was so excessive that it threatened the overthrow of [the] very moral and social nature amongst us. In former days we had witnessed the withering and blighting influences of this monster evil on society. We have seen him enter the quiet and happy home circle and with one stroke of his arm of iron dash in pieces the family alter and take up his abode where peace and love had hovered so long. We have seen society wither under his scorching breath and the hopes of many a fond mother crushed and end in despair. We have seen all the tender sensibilities of man's nature destroyed and his heart steeped in the very fumes [of] hell by this agent of evil. And here again while strangers in a strange land and in prison we behold his desolating

---

inquiry suggested the conclusion. Nothing, however, was further from my mind. Had I not deferred to the advise of some around me, and followed the bent of my inclination by inserting only a clause or two as it regards my personal feelings, there would have been no misunderstanding. My only remedy now, is a letter of explanation, which I have already addressed to Col. Purnell.

Prayers at the usual hour, and but few in attendance. Quite a crowd in our room to-night [sic]. Got to bed late, with a mind ill at rest.

[5] Sutlers were civilian merchants who sold provisions to the army. Sutlers would travel by wagon with the armies selling all manner of goods to the soldiers. The sutlers were permitted inside Fort Delaware to sell goods to both the prisoners and the soldiers.

effects. The only apparent bond of union amongst us was our devotion to the cause of our common country, and this was too weak to stand the test of the monster in many instances, and personal difficulties were of frequent occurrence. This traffic was carried on solely for the sake of gain and daily we witnessed the sad spectacle of seeing the souls of our fellow men placed in human balances and weighed against gold and silver. Would that we could stop here but other kindred vices no less degrading in the eyes of an all wise God were practiced increasingly. Gambling in all its forms were practiced without mitigation. The gambling tables were set in every Division[6] room. Surrounded by the unfortunate viceing [sic] to his habit from morning until a late hour at night. Cursing was the common dialect of the camp. At almost every breath we could hear the name of the Lord God in vain. The number of professing Christians; afterwards found to be forty, were scarcely known or recognized as such. They yielded in a greater or less degree to the influences around them. They met infrequently could be seen around the gaming tables interested in the varying fortunes of the gambler. Some went so far as to participate in the games. It is however important to state that there was a few who stood aloof from these vices and whose hearts were daily lifted to God for a revival of Christian piety in our midst.

---

[6]The prisoners in the fort were segregated into individual areas, known as "Divisions." At its peak, there were at least 34 Divisions at Fort Delaware.

The man of God thus beholding the desolation of our Zion could but exclaim in the anguish of his soul. "There is more that seeketh [sic] after God." They are all gone out of the way. They are together become unprofitable. There is none that death good no not one. This brief illusion to the universal prevalence of wickedness among the impertinent and lukewarmness [sic] among believers will suffice to show our extreme moral desolation. Among the forty Christians before mentioned there was one minister Captain A.M. Samford[7] [sic] of 14th Texas Cavalry. He had labored for the good of souls at Camp Chase but failed to arouse believers from the deadly sin of apathy which had had seized their hearts. But he was not despondent. Like a faithful sentinel on the watch towers of Zion he continue to labor.

On Sunday morning, April 3rd [1864] division service was held for the first time in division 29. The audience was silent and attentive while Captain Samford [sic] preached from the following text. Thou shall love thy God with all thy heart and with all thy soul and with all thy strength and with all thy mind and thy neighbors as thyself. He showed they necessity of devoting our lives to the device of God and presenting our bodies as a living sacrifice through our Lord and Savior Jesus Christ. In the evening Capt. Samford [sic] preached

---

[7] Captain Alexander M. Sanford served in Company "G" of the 14th Texas Confederate Cavalry, also known as "Johnson's Mounted Volunteers."

again in Division 27 from Zech 4:6[8]. In the conclusion of his second discourse an event occurred which subsequently led to great results. The Rev. Dr. Isaac W.H. [sic] Handy[9] of Portsmouth, VA was permitted to visit our barracks from the fort where he had suffered a painful imprisonment for more than nine months for conscience sake.[10] At the request of many preached from Jere. 17th 9[th][11]: The

---

[8] Zechariah 4:6 – "Then he answered and spake unto me, saying, This is the word of the Lord unto Zerubbabel, saying, Not by might, nor by power, but by my spirit, saith the Lord of hosts." (King James translation).

[9] See Appendix B for a biographical sketch of Dr. Isaac W.K. Handy

[10] **Handy Diary: Sunday, April 3, 1864: At about ten o'clock this morning, a messenger came to the door, with an order from Gen. Schoepf, for "Dr. Handy to call at his office." Immediately complying with the order, I found Gen. Vance had preceded me, and was awaiting my arrival, in conversation with the Commandant, and Capt. Ahl. They were talking about an arrangement for preaching, at the barracks. They were talking about an arrangement for preaching, at the barracks. After a little pleasantry, in which I was cautioned not to encourage escapes, and to do what I could to "convert" the Rebels, Gen. Schoepf handed me a parole of the island, with permission to be out "from reveille, to retreat." Accompanying Gen. Vance to his quarters, we there agreed upon 4 o'clock P.M., as a suitable hour for service.**

At the appointed hour I walked over to the place of preaching accompanied by Generals Thompson and Vance, Colonels Duke, Coleman, Morgan, Tucker and Ward, and Lieut. Smith, a young officer on the staff of Gen. Vance. No previous notice had been given, and two services had already been held, during the morning and afternoon. All seemed ready, however, for another sermon, and preparations were made immediately, by circulating the notice and arranged the seats. The "division" to be used was occupied by the officers of Morgan's command, lately from the Ohio Penitentiary. In a very short time the apartment was entirely filled – benches, bunks, and every available standing-place – with intelligent and noble looking young men. I

was introduced to the assembly by the Rev. Mr. Sanford, a "Rebel" captain, who being a Methodist minister, is officiating as chaplain to Morgan's Brigade. I have not had such an audience since I have been on the Island; and for intelligence and fine appearance, and all males, not for many a day past. I preached about three quarters of an hour, on the desperate wickedness of the heart. The attention was profound to the last moment. Not a single man left during the sermon, nor did the slightest interruption occur. It was a decidedly pleasant time; and I thank God for the opportunity of proclaiming the truths of His Word to a congregation so unusually interesting.

After preaching, a number of officers came forward, seeking introduction through Gen. Vance and Col. Duke; others had been introduced before the services. Among those whose acquaintance I had the pleasure of forming were Major Bullock, brother of the Rev. Dr. Bullock, of Baltimore; Major Steel, son-in-law of Rev. Dr. R.J. Breckenridge; Major Kilgore, Adjutant-general on the staff of General Ector, of Texas; Major Lamar Fontaine, the reputed author of "All Quiet along the Potomac;" Capt. Charlton and Col. Dick Morgan, brothers to the General, besides various others whose names I cannot now recall. One young man held me very cordially by the hand, stating that he recently had a good deal of affliction, and that he had experienced a change of heart during his imprisonment at Columbus. He also requested an opportunity for a private interview as soon as convenient.

The quarters occupied by these officers, with the building and fence, constitute a sort of Pen, with an area of about two acres. The long side of the building and the parallel fence are each about 300 feet, running east and west; and the two ends are severally about half that length. The Campus is low and flat, and at this time quiet muddy from the recent rains. Intersecting walks, constructed of planks, are arranged at proper distance, and add greatly to the comfort of those who would seek exercise in bad weather. The quarters seem to be ample for the present number of prisoners, the bunks wide and comfortable, and the "division" well heated. One large stove appears to be sufficient for the shelter occupied by the Morgan me.

By request of Capt. Samford, notice was given that I would preach, Deo volente, at the same place, at 10 o'clock on next Sabbath.

Our usual evening services were held in [barracks] No. 2, with an increased attendance. Omitted the lecture; a chapter; made a few practical remarks; had one hymn; and closed with the doxology; sung in a standing position."

heart is deceitful above all things and desperately wicked. Thus in our first Sabbath at Fort Delaware had past away, a third sermon had been delivered. Not withstanding, the Giver of all goods had so bountifully blest us with the means of grave. It is said to state that while these services were being conducted, the card table was set and well attended in other Divisions in violation of the plain language of the Decalogue "Remember the Sabbath day to keep it holy [12] " during the insuring week these three sermons were productive of no results that were perceptible. Our condition remained as previously depicted but steps were taken to around believers from their lethargy.

At the suggestion of Dr. Handy a roll of the church members was made when it was found that only forty had reported their names. On Saturday the 9th of April [1864] a number of Testaments Episcopal prayer books tract's and religious papers were sent into the barracks for distribution [13]. Dr. Handy was permitted to visit us again on

---

11 Jeremiah 17:9 – "The heart is deceitful above all things, and desperately wicked: who can know it?" (King James translation)

12 Exodus 20:8 – "Remember the sabbath day, to keep it holy." (King James translation)

13 Religious groups located in nearby communities would periodically send prayer books and religious tracts into the fort.

Sunday[14] the 10th [of] April [1864] and preached a very interesting and instructive sermon from 1st Cor 9th 24[th][15] "So run that you may

---

[14] Handy Diary: Sunday, April 10, 1864: We had a terrible storm last night, which drove the water over the banks all around the Island. At Post No. 12, the sentry stood knee deep in the water until relieved by another who was not quiet so literal in the interpretation of orders. Two men, who were trying to make their way to the privy by adjusting some boards across certain low places were hailed by the sentinel, but not hearing the call, were shot. Neither of them were killed, and one only is reported badly wounded. I have not learned further particulars, except that the men were Tennesseans.

At 10 o'clock, in company with Gen. Vance, Cols. Duke and Coleman, Capt. Morgan, and my room-mate Brogden, I repaired to the barracks, to hold another Sabbath morning service with the others. The congregation was not quiet so large as on last Sabbath, but the room was well filled, and had a pleasant time. I preached from I. Cor. Ix, 24, "so runs that ye may obtain." Gen. Vance and Major Bullock, with other officers, sat near the stand, and acted as a sort of choir. The Chaplain, Capt. Samford, did not come forward until after the services were over.

On leaving "the Pen," a young man approached me, and extending his hand, said he: ---

"I heard your sermon and listened attentively. You told us that a man might be a lawyer, a physician, soldier, or anything else, and serve God righteously as such, provided, the duties of his profession or occupation are performed with an eye single to His glory. Now, sir, I am a lawyer, and I want to know why a gambler has not as much right to serve God as any other man."
I had, in the course of my sermon, alluded indirectly to the vice of card-playing, and the question was evidently proposed with a sort of exultant air, to catch me with my own words.

"If it were true, as I had suggested, that secular duties were religious duties, when attended to at the right time and in the right place, why," said he, "could not a man, as an amusement, indulge a little in gambling?"
"It is impossible," I replied, "to serve God and be a gambler. The two things are wholly incompatible."

"Does the Bible say anything about gambling, or card playing?" he rejoined.

"It is true," I answered "that the word of God is silent, in regard to the specific vice of card playing; but the principle involved is clearly revealed, and there can be no question about the sin."

"Well, sir," he again inquired, "tell me, how you make it a sin?"

The sin, I assured him, did not consist in the mere tossing and arranging of a number of painted cards, but in the waste of time, idle words, profane swearing, drinking, brawls, fights, dishonesty, and other ills, which, so constantly, attend the practice.

"Then, upon the same principle, you may denounce the business of merchandising, or any other pursuit of life, because men choose to be dishonest, or otherwise to commit evil, in connection with their various occupations."

"By no means! for sin has not necessary connection with these, Card playing, on the other hand, is seldom or never unattended with one or more of these acknowledged evils. Even "playing for fun" as it is called has the 'appearance of evil' – which the Apostle denounces and it is rarely the case, that those who play merely fro amusement, do not presently put up a small sum, to add interest to the game; and thus sooner or later, from the fascination of the sport or rom love of gain, involve themselves to such an extent, as to be guilty in the long run of all the attendant sins."

"Well," said he, "I love God; and I think I can serve God quiet as well as any other man."

At this point, the conversation ended; and as he turned to leave me, placing my hand upon his shoulder, I remarked, "I hope, my friend, you will see, ere long, that it is utterly impossible for a gambler to be a true servant of God."

A crowd had gathered around; and I learned from one of the company, that my lawyer friend was one of the most noted card players in "the Pen."
The young man, who on last Sabbath, sought a private interview, was Capt. W.C.S. _____, of Texas.

Whilst the gentleman was came with me, were moving around among their friends, I had an opportunity for a full talk with him. He told me that he had been piously educated, and that his parents were Presbyterian. His conscience had reproved him for neglected opportunities; but he never experience any

obtain." At this meeting he announced his purpose to preach for us every Sunday if agreeable and also that he had effected arrangements to visit us during the week at which time he would be

---

special seriousness, until he found himself a prisoner in the Ohio Penitentiary. Here got hold of Nelson's "Cause and Cure of Infidelity," and although not a sceptic [sic] in regard to Divine teaching, he felt himself to be a sinner, and the book was well adapted to him in his distressed condition. His convictions increased with such power, that he could do nothing but read the word of God, and talk upon religious subjects. His companions thought he was losing his mind and advised him to lay the Bible aside. They all jeered and tormented him to such an extend, that it was a relief to him to get into his cell, and there in his loneliness, commune with God in prayer. Under these circumstances, and calling to mind the teaching of his good mother, he at length found peace in believing.

Capt. S. tells me, the trouble now is, that with the consciousness of great shortcoming, he fears he is presuming too much. He also complains of difficulties in his way, from his surrounding at the barracks. He was anxious to know what course he should pursue, to avoid the appearance of ostentation in his devotions – there being no opportunity in the "pen" for a moment's privacy. I advised him, under all the circumstances, to make a closet of his bunk; but not to shrink from an open and regular perusal of the Word. I suggested, in this connection, that God might have some work for him to perform, in the way of usefulness to others; and if so, he should not turn from it. He admitted the probability, and expressed a desire to study theology, for his own edification and comfort. It is not unlikely, that this young man, who had been "led by a way he knew not," may yet become an honored servant of Christ, preaching liberty to the captives.

I met with two other young men, who introduced themselves as belonging to Presbyterian families, and as old acquaintances of shorter catechism. One of them, Lieut. Andrews, is a step-son of the Rev. Dr. Mitchell, of Florence, Ala., who was four months a prisoner under the Lincoln rule, because he could not make just such prayers in the pulpit as suited the men in power.

Services in [barracks] No. 2 at the usual hour. Preached Christ to the accustomed few.

---

[15] 1 Corrinthians 9:24 – "Know ye not that they which run in a race run all, but one receiveth the prize? So run, that ye may obtain." (King James translation)

27

happy to converse with any who felt an interest in their souls salvation if they would but let him know who they were. He urged Christians to go to work and labor for the good of souls. Pointing to our field of labor he would with the deepest interest speak of the good that might be accomplished if we would labor as it becometh [sic] good soldiers of the cross. The manifestation of this interesting our welfare began to beget an interest in the hearts of the Christians and a few were aroused to a more active discharge of their duties. But the influence on the unconverted was so far imperceptible as will be shown hereafter. The first evidence of an increased interest in religion was the organized at the suggestion of Capt. W.C. Shane who had found Jesus so precious to his soul while in close confinement at the Ohio penitentiary. There alone in his cell, the truth of God penetrated his soul and he was brought to a knowledge of the truth as it is in Christ Jesus. His conference Capt. Samford on this subject resulted in the determination of holding prayer meetings nightly which at first was conducted privately but few of the brethren having knowledge of its existence. The first meeting was held on the night of night of April the 11th [1864][16] and was

---

[16] **Handy Diary: Monday, April 11, 1864: Major Fontaine sent me a copy of his "Dream Thoughts while in Prison," which I wish to preserve fro his own sake, as well as the intrinsic value of the poetry. I saw him yesterday on his return from the hospital to the barracks. He is walking with a crutch, on account of a wound received in battle, and which is not yet healed. The Major has seen much service, and has been wounded thirteen times. He was shot five**

participated in by Maj. Bullock, Capt. Tracy, Capt. Bennett, Capt. Moore, Capt. Moses in addition to the brethren already mentioned. The division in which these meetings were held was destitute of stove and benches and the weather was disagreeably cold. But these faithful brethren were not to be deterred from their labor but

---

times while acting as a scout for Gen. Pemberton. He was the only one of Pemberton's scouts that succeeded in getting through to Gen. Johnston, on the Big Black River. For his gallantry, and suffering, he was promoted from the ranks to his present position, by Gen. Johnston. On the arrival of Major Fontaine, at Fort Delaware, he was offered a parole of the island, by Gen. Schoepf, with permission also to visit Philadelphia; but he declined the privilege, preferring to remain in closer confinement, with his brother officers.

Reports having reached the ears of Gen. Schoepf, that certain Rebel officers have been imbibing too freely, he visited their quarters on last Sunday, and with a paper in hand, which had called his attention to the subject, he made a little address, at the table, in somewhat the following style: --

"There now, gentleman! You see how it is – I am obliged to notice the matter. I know that a little of the 'ardent" is necessary to keep soul and body together; and I have given the sutler orders to let you have it. But you must not get drunk. If anybody, however, does get too much, you must not let him walk about 'the pen.' I want you to take him to his bunk immediately; and you must keep him there until he gets sober." This good-natured, but rather too indulgent speech, from the "old Hungarian," made him a popular man, at least for one day; and three cheers having been proposed, were given with a good will, for Gen. Schoepf.

As an off-set to this lecture, my friend Tibbetts soliloquizes:

> "Brandy, brandy, bane of life!
> Spring of tumult, source of strife!
> Could I half thy courses tell,
> The wise would have thee safe in hell!"

The Confederate officers have had their money returned. The General says it is not worth much, and they can have it to play enchre with.

continue to meet each other promptly at the place appointed, however, inclement the night. Their devotions to Almighty God ascended to heaven. The earnest petitions of these disciples of our Lord were unitedly [sic] borne to a throne of grace for a revival of religion in our prison. And most graciously did He bless their efforts. These meetings were soon generally known and were quiet largely attended and in preparations to the increase of attendants the deeper and more extended was the interest manifested. During the first week of May[17] [1864] the meeting was so largely attended and

---

[17] Handy Diary: Sunday, May 8, 1864: This has been the most active day I have spent on the island. And I may add, the most interesting, and perhaps the most pregnant of results. I preached to the officers at 10 A.M., from I Cor. 21: "Ye cannot drink of the cup of the Lord and of the cup of devils; ye cannot be partakers of the Lord's table and the table of devils." We had a full house. The attention was earnest to the last. After the benediction, numbers remained for conversation and advice. Capt. White and Lieut. Caldwell were examined, with a view to a seat at the Lord's table; and were advised to come forward. Capt. H.H.M. _____ ;, gave evidence of the great change, but hesitates about an open profession at this time. Lieuts. Hardee and Cyrus responded to an invitation for those who have never been baptized, but who was hoping in Christ, to make it known. After examination, there were requested to present themselves this afternoon. Capt. D. _____, Lieuts. B. _____ and A. _____, and others, church members of long standing, but lately cold and backsliding, were encouraged in view of their manifest penitence, to renew their covenant at the table of the Lord. Some old professors seemed to be established; and one lately converted in the Ohio Penitentiary, told me that he could think of scarcely anything, night or day, but the subject of religion. He said that Christ was precious to him beyond measure; and that he would wish no greater happiness than to gaze upon His gaze upon His face, through an endless eternity.

In the afternoon, we assembled to celebrate the death and suffering of our blessed Redeemer. Forty-four persons had handed in their names as professors of religion, of different denominations. There were publically

30

the interest so increased that it was thought advisable to extend the privileges and blessing more fully to the unconverted. Accordingly on May the 9th [1864][18] an invitation was extended to all who felt an

---

announced, that they might be better known to one another, and a closer intimacy established. The services were commenced with singing, prayer, and appropriate Scripture reading. An address was delivered, explanatory of the nature of the ordinance; and illustrative of the obligation involved in the Saviour's [sic] command. "Do this in remembrance of me." Great solemnity prevailed; and many tears by strong men, and gallant soldiers. Hardee, Cyrus, White, and Caldwell, in a standing posture, responded to certain questions, with a view to a public expression of their faith in Christ. The first two were baptized, as they still stood erect; and the four, in answer to the usual interrogatories, solemnly avouched the Lord to be their God.

To relieve the services from every sectarian bias, persons of various denominations were requested to assist in the distribution of the bread and wine; all of them being officers in their respective churches. These persons were Capt. A.M. Samford, Methodist; Capt. C.L. Bennett, Baptist; and Lieut. F.C. Moore, Presbyterian. During the circulation of the sacred elements, a profound silence prevailed. At the close of the distribution, the communicants were requested to engage for a few moments, in silent prayer to God, asking strength and blessing for themselves, under the present now and trying circumstances; and for each other things as they might desire for their families and others. It was an interesting occasion; every man arose, and responded a cordial amen to his heart, to this audible expression from their fellow prisoner pastor. The entire services were concluded with the dedication hymn:

"Lord, I am thine, entirely thine"

the whole congregation rising, and the communicates joining with a full and earnest expression, which told that their hearts were stirred with them.

Thus passed this precious Sabbath. May the good work be continued, until many souls shall be brought in the Kingdom.

[18]   Handy Diary: Monday, May 9, 1864: How Company Q managed to endure their old quarters, is inexplicable. The Politicals, certainly, have not managed so well. The bed-bugs have swarmed upon them beyond endurance.

Failing after the most preserving efforts to accomplish anything in the way of subduring the enemy., boisterous complaints were made, and orders were given this morning for a general inundation of the building. Hose and pipes were introduced through the ceilings, and it was not long before the water was pouring in heavy streams, from the lofts, cuddies, bunks, and every other conceivable rendezvous of the multitudinous horde. Of course, every man had to do the best he could for himself, in the protection of his "dud." These were scattered all about the interior of the fort; and the "animals" so lately caged, and guarded, were wandering here and there about the casemates, hunting quarters, and promising themselves at least one good night's rest in the open air. Suffering from a violent headache, I had retreated for a time to No. 6, in hope of relief by a short nap. The announcement was soon made, that all my old associates were being removed to the barracks. On going down, I found but a single man left to tell the tale;; and notwithstanding the number of very pleasant fellows around me, in the persons of Generals, Colonels, Captains, and Lieutenants, I really felt, for a time, as if I had been deserted by all my friends. If they have gone to the officer's quarters, they will have no cause to regret the change. Had not this relief from bed-bugs been afforded, a plan to burn the building would certainly have been executed to-night.

My sickness continued all day, and towards evening the pain became intense. Gen. Vance and others were very kind in their attentions. Mustard was applied to my forehead, temples, and the back of my head, and my feet soaked in hot water. Nothing seemed to do me much good, until the stomach was relieved by a glass of milk-warm water, and the nerves quieted by a good sleep. These headaches are almost inseparably connected with my Sabbath labors, especially after scenes of special interest and excitement.

Capt. Gibson is enjoying a visit from his wife. General Schoepf has been very kind in extending him this privilege; and apologizes that the condition of his own family is such, at this time, that he cannot have Mrs. G. at his house. Gibson is a very clever fellow, a graduate of both Yale and Heidelberg, and very much of a gentleman. His wife is a daughter of Henry Duncan, Esq., of Kentucky, and as I understand by her sister, Miss D., and the party are putting up for the present, at the island hotel.

A flaming heading appears in the Philadelphia *Inquirer* of to-day, proclaiming great victories for the Federal armies on the Potomac. A few years hence the papers of this will, no doubt, be a literary curiousity. Is not this the age of mendacity?

interest in their souls [sic] eternal welfare and desired God's people to pray for them to come forward and let the fact be known. Four mourners came forward in response to this call. Thus the hearts of Christians were made to rejoice. On the day following[19] the same

---

[19] Handy Diary: Tuesday, May 10, 1864: We have had several days of unusually fine weather. The Delaware river has been as smooth as glass – while vessels have appeared as usual, in every direction. Visited the officer's quarters, and found the political prisoners located in the vicinity of the west gate, next door to the sutler, who has established himself in "the pen," near the bank. Regretted to notice several of the Politicals but just recovering from a heavy "drunk," and was informed that a number of officers had joined with them in the spree. Altogether, they have had a "high old time." Among the first whom I discovered in a state of intoxication, was one in whom I felt special interest, and who promised me weeks ago never to touch the poison again. How often it is that a "man resolves, and resolves, and yet does the same."

The awakening continues. A number of persons have, publicly, expressed an interest on the subject of religion – among them are Capt. H.H.M. _____, and Lieuts. J.H. _____, J.M. _____, and R.T. _____, with all of whom I have had free conversations, and find them not far from the Kingdom of Heaven. I have advised them according to their several phases of experience, and pray God to lead them in the way of all truth.

The two pens, occupied severally by officers and privates, are separated by fences, which stand about fifteen or twenty feet apart. These fences are guarded by sentinels, who perambulate an elevated platform, from which they may overlook the two enclosures. It requires considerable dexterity to elude the watchfulness of the rough "blue coats," who are there night and day. The cunning "Rebs" have found an expedient, in every pebble of suitable weight to secure the necessary impetus for communication across the parapet. Notes are constantly falling into the area on the officer's side, complaining of hard usage by the Yankee authorities, and asking help or redress from the Confederate leaders. To-day, one of the little carrier pigeons brought the following to Gen. Vance:

To Gen. ROBERT B. VANCE,
          Or any other Rebel Officer:

33

invitation was extended but ere Capt. [Alexander M.] Samford could end his earnest appeal for all to come and live, the mustering was dispersed by the Federal authorities and all present informed that meeting for religious worship would be prohibited in future until further orders. Thus at a time when our meeting were being

---

Prompted by the gnawing of hunger, I am emboldened to make this appeal to you; hoping that being informed of our suffering, you can and will appeal to the Commanding General in our behalf, and if possible have our rations increased.

For breakfast we get one-fifth of a loaf of bread, and from four to six ounces of meat – fresh or salt beef, or both – and a pint of very inferior coffee. For dinner we get the same amount of break and meat – Sunday and Wednesday excepted – when, instead of meat, we get two or three potatoes, and a cup of bean or rice soup. As to supper, we have none.
Whether the rations are allowed us by the authorities and wasted by the cooks, I cannot say, as I do not know. But one thing is certain, we are suffering.

Respectfully,
A HUNGRY REBEL

This note was handed to Gen. Vance, who, feeling it to be his duty to do so, presented it to Gen. Schoepf. The immediate reply was: "Say to them, for their consolation – *the rations are to be resolved.*"

The authorities are "shutting down" upon the prisoners, in every part of the island. Officers and privates are, alike, subject to the rigors of this change. Rations are to be reduced; paroles are to be restricted; and there are strong indications of an entirely new order of things. A notice has been struck up to the hall, in regard to a more systematic, and regular prisoners of war on parole, to very circumscribed limits, and disallowing all intercourse between them and the officers at the barracks.

Unfavorably news by the "grape vine!" The Yankees are encouraged!

Heard a musket fire, and noticed a great running towards the barracks. What is the matter?

especially blest by the outpouring of God's love and mercy by an intervention of human authority there were discontinued. Up to this point Dr. Handy had been visiting us regularly during the week conducting our prayer meeting and conversing with all on the subject of religion who winced an interest on the subject. In the mean time the religious element was largely on the increase. The sale of spirituous liquors had in a measure been stopped. Gambling to a considerable extent had abated. Swearing was still common but to a considerable extent checked by the religious influence brought to bear, it will not be proper to state in this connection that sometime prior to this, a library of several hundred volumes known as the prisoners library at Fort Delaware had been sent to us by the ladies of Philadelphia[20] which proved a valuable auxiliary to those who were laboring so earnestly for a reformation in our barracks. Those who had been seen at the card tables on the Lord [sic] Day being now supplied with reading matter devoted Sundays to reading and attending divine services. Many brethren had wandered far from the path of duty and had become so blinded by the "god of this" world that they had forgotten. They were purged from their old sins were brought back to the fold of Christ and began labor afresh in His vineyard. The influence on the unconverted was much greater than

---

[20] The "Ladies of Philadelphia" was a woman's society formed during the Revolutionary War whose original purpose was the relief of Revolutionary War soldiers who were in need of clothing. This philanthropic effort was carried on during the Civil War as the ladies sought to bring comfort to the Confederate soldiers imprisoned just across the river from Philadelphia at Fort Delaware.

was at first supposed. Some who had not presented themselves publically as subjects of prayer had made their requests known to their friends privately. Others communicated their convictions of sin in writing and asked an interest in the prayers of the Church. These communications being always read at the prayer meeting. Such was the state of religious feeling in our midst when we were prohibited from assembling ourselves together to worship the Giver of every good and perfect gift.

We know ask you to go back with us two days, prior to the suppression of the public worship of God by the federal while we dwell for a moment on the First Communion of the Disciples of Christ at Fort Delaware.

On Sunday morning May 8th [1864] as usual Dr. Hamby was admitted to our barracks and preached from the following text[21]: Ye

---

[21] **Handy Diary: Sunday May 8, 1864: This has been the most active day I have spent on the island; and I may add, the most interesting, and perhaps the most pregnant of results. I preached to the officers at 10 A.M., from 1 Cor. 21:** *"Ye cannot drink of the Lord and of the cup of devils; ye cannot be partakers of the Lord's table and the table of devils."* **We had a full house. The attention was earnest to the last. After the benediction, numbers remained for conversation and advice. Capt. White and Lieut. Caldwell were examined, with a view to a seat at the Lord's table; and were advised to come forward. Capt. H.H.M. _____ gave evidence of the great change, but hesitates about an open profession at this time. Lieuts. Hardee and Cyrus responded to an invitation for those who have never been baptized, but who are hoping in Christ, to make it known. After examination, they were requested to present themselves this afternoon. Capt. D. _____, Lieuts. B. _____ and A. _____, and**

others, church members of long standing, but lately cold and backsliding, were encouraged in view of their manifest penitence, to renew their covenant at the table of the Lord. Some old professors seemed to be established; and one lately converted in the Ohio Penitentiary, told me that he could now think of scarcely anything, night or day, but the subject of religion. He said that Christ was precious to him beyond measure; and that he would wish no greater happiness than to gaze upon His face, through an endless eternity.

In the afternoon, we assembled to celebrate the death and suffering of our blessed Redeemer. Forty-four persons had handed in their names as professors of religion, of different denominations. These were publicly announced, that they might be better know to one another, and a closer intimacy established. The services were commenced with singing, prayer, and appropriate Scripture reading. An address was delivered, explanatory of the nature of the ordinance; and illustrative of the obligation involved in the Saviour's command, *"Do this in remembrance of me."* Great solemnity prevailed; and many tears were shed by strong men, and gallant soldiers. Hardee, Cyrus, White and Caldwell, in a standing posture, responded to certain questions, with a view to a public expression of their faith in Christ. The first two were baptized, as they still stood erect; and the four, in answer to the usual interrogatories, solemnly avouched the Lord to be their God.

To relived the services from every sectarian bias, persons of various denominations were requested to assist in the distribution of the bread and wine; all of them being officers in their respective churches. These persons were Capt. A.M. Samford, Methodist; Capt. C.L. Bennett, Baptist; and Lieut. F.C. Moore, Presbyterian. During the circulation of the sacred elements, a profound silence prevailed. At the close of the distribution, the communicants were requested to engage for a few moments, in silent prayer to God, asking strength and blessing themselves, under the present new and trying circumstances; and for such other things as they might desire for their families and others. It was an interesting occasion; every man arose, and responded a cordial *amen* in his heart, to this audible expression from their fellow prisoners pastor. The entire services were concluded with the dedication hymn:

"Lord, I am thine, entirely thine"

the whole congregation rising, and the communicants joining with a full and earnest expression, which told their whole hearts were stirred within them.

37

cannot drink the cup of the Lord and the cup of the devils. Ye cannot be partakers of the Lord's table and the table of the devils.: 1st Cor 10th 21 [22]. Our venerable brother dwelt at length on Christian consistency urging with great earnestness and zeal that the followers of Christ should avoid even the very appearance of evil. That they should deny themselves all worldly lusts and cleave to that which was good as it becometh [sic] the peculiar people of God. At the conclusion of the sermon all Christians of whatever denominations were invited to meet with the brethren in the evening and commemorate the suffering and death of our Savior at the communion table. An invitation was also given to any who had experience a change of heart and had not connected themselves with any church to come forward and be received into the church at large if they desired it. Also any who desired to received the ordinances of baptism to make their request known and it could be attended to at once. At the time appointed in the evening a large and attentive audience had assembled to witness the disciples partake of the emblems of the brethren body and shed blood of our Lord and Savior Jesus Christ.

Thus passed this precious Sabbath. May the good work be continued, until many souls be brought into the Kingdom.

[22] 1 Corinthians 10:21 – "Ye cannot drink the cup of the Lord, and the cup of devils: ye cannot be partakers of the Lord's table, and of the table of devils." (King James Translation)

The following brethren made application for admission into the Church and were unanimously received into full fellowship: Capt. W.R. White of Ark., Lieut. J.F. Caldwell of Mo., Lieut. T.P. Hardee of Ga., Adjt. C.V. Cyrus of Tenn. The two latter brethren were at their request baptized according to the custom of the Presbyterian Church. After a short discussion from Dr. Hamby explanatory of the institution they were about to observe urging each one to examine himself and so let him eat the elements were produced and administrated to the brethren in a sitting posture. The patriarchal appearance of Dr. Handy, his deeply fervent tones as he repeated the words of his Master, "Take eat this is My body" and the tearful eyes and the bowed heads of the communicants as the loafs and cups were passed amongst them, made this a most solemn and interesting scene. It cannot soon be forgotten by those witnessed it. This meeting was not only a solemn and interesting one but it proved beneficial as a means of "groth in grace." The announcement that an opportunity would be afforded for all Christians to meet in holy communion around the sacramental board was made more than a week prior to its observance.

The announcement crowded the Christian's memory with the joys and blessing bestowed on him by his Heavenly Father in former days while showing forth the Lord's death till he comes in the observances of this Holy institution and he paused and looked within himself and searched his heart as a with a lighted candle. Dr. Handy visited the barracks twice during the preceding week and conversed with many on the subject of this communion, urging them to make a most rigid self-examination and to engage continually in prayer to God. By this means the brethren were fully aroused and saw themselves in their prayer light and as they moved among their comrades they began to scatter broadcast the seeds of life, and while some fell by the way side and in stony places others fell in good ground and brought forth fruit to the honor and glory of God.

We now resume our narrative where we left off, the prohibition of public worship by the Federal authorities, the regular prayer meetings were again commenced on Sunday, May the 14th [1864] Capt. Shane and others having obtained permission to continue public worship in a different division. On Sunday, May 15th [23]

---

[23] **Handy Diary: Sunday May 15, 1864: Had much difficulty this morning, in deciding whether I should make an effort to visit the officers' quarters, without seeing the General; or, assuming that the late order did not include myself, I should venture again, upon my old pass. Concluded to see Gen. Schepf, and learn whether I am to understand him as interdicting my visits, and thus putting an end to the preaching. He received me with less affability than usual; and, in reply to my inquiry, informed me, that "everything is closed up," – adding, "I am acting under orders." This settled the matter, at once, and I returned to my casemate, regretting that a door of usefulness had thus been closed; but feeling that I had done my duty, and leaving the result to God.**

I was reclining in my bunk, thinking about the present restrictions, and doubting whether I was better off, with or without my parole – when Cunningham came in, and announced that Capt. Gordon, Capt. Noel, Dr. Lee

[1864], there was no preaching in the barracks, Dr. Handy being prohibited from visiting as usual and Capt. Samford thinking it best owing to the recent interference by the authorities to omit services on that day. In the evening of the same day, however, Dr. Handy and the political prisoners confined in the Fort were sent into our barracks and assigned quarters. The great laborer was thus ushered in to the harvest field. He was not transferred to the midst of those for whose spiritual welfare he was so much concerned and for whom he labored so devotedly. If the three days interruption of religious services checked the good work which had commenced, the accession of Dr. Handy to those engaged in it more than compensated for the lost ground. Indeed, the daily intercourse of this venerable brother among us was productive of great spiritual good. He believe wherever God sent him, there he intended for him to labor. So he entered with all his mind and strength into the work before him. Prayer meeting was held on this same evening conducted by him; and at which the first conversion was announced.

---

and Dr. Handy must get ready to remove to the barracks, immediately. We were soon packed up; and followed the sergeant to our new quarters outside of the fort. I found that the political prisoners had been removed from their first locality; and were now occupying "Chebang" No. 26. Several strangers had followed them in, whom I found to be regular gamblers, seeking prey.

After all, the good providence of God is apparent. At the usual hour for evening services, I met a crowd of hearers, and preached from Heb. Xi. 3, " *How shall we escape, if we neglect so great salvation?"* A solemn and attentive audience; and the Word, evidently, received with gladness. Was assisted by several brethren, who led in prayer. A work of grace is still in progress.

On May the 19th [1864], one hundred and sixty officers captured during the [B]attle of the [W]ilderness[24] arrived and confined in our barracks[25]. Among them were many brethren and one minister, Capt.

---

[24] The Battle of the Wilderness, fought May 5-7, 1864, in present day Spotsylvania and Orange County, Virginia, was a clash between the armies of Ulysses Grant and Robert E. Lee.

[25] **Handy Diary: Tuesday, May 17, 1864: Another change! In prospect of the coming of a large reinforcement of officers, we were ordered, this morning, to vacate division 27, and move into 23. By this arrangement, we have gained considerably. We have a larger room, and a better locality—giving us more shade, ampler space, and a greater proximity to "the rear", which, even now, is only reached by one hundred and fifty steps.**

At about four o'clock, the expected reinforcement arrived, numbering one hundred and eighty-four officers—Colonels, Majors, Captains, Lieutenants. Maj. Gen. Edward Johnson, and Brig. Gen. George H. Stewart are, also, on the island, in our quarters, in the interior of the Fort, and have accepted paroles. We are greatly surprised at the appearance of the crowd, after so much exposure, and fatigue. A more healthy looking set of men I have not seen. They are all dirty, of course; but not ragged. They seem, generally, to be in good spirits, and bring cheering accounts from the front. One hundred officers were left at Point Lookout. They came under strong guard, but were treated with respect.

Was invited to dine with the gentlemen of Morgan's Division. In consequences of the new arrivals, considerable confusion occurred among the messes, at the table. These gentlemen were exceedingly generous in dividing their stores among the new-comers; but we had enough left for ourselves, including plenty of fine ham and blackberry preserves; and might have forgotten our prison, for a moment, had we not noticed hundreds around us restricted to the course and unpalatable fare of the common table.
Held the accustomed meeting, at No. 31. The large room was filled with earnest worshippers. Subject of discourse: The willingness of Christ to receive even the greatest sinners.

Several gentlemen called in to see me—among whom was Capt. Buford A. Tracy, of Morgan's command. This officer is a member of the Old School

T.W. Harris[26] of the 12th Ga. The church members immediately enrolled their names and active participated in our religious exercises. Capt. Harris also began to labor in the capacity of a minister.

On Friday, May the 20th [1864], an inquiry meeting was organized at the suggestion of Dr. Handy[27]. These meetings were held every

---

Baptist Church, and, evidently, an earnest Christian. He gave us a detailed account of the manner in which Gen. Morgan made his escape. It took nineteen days, for about twenty men, working eight hours each day, to cut through the cemented pavement, dig the earth tunnel, and penetrate the two walls, each about three feet in thickness. The tools with which they worked were old knives, and a fire shovel. The working band was thoroughly organized, and many of their own number were not informed of the secret. Capt. Tracy, generally, acted as watchman, and designated the approach of danger, by a peculiar cough, or clearing of the throat. The attention of the sentinels, in the long passage, was drawn off by the anecdotes, "yarns," dancing, and such other means as they could resort tom as the result proved, with the greatest success. Seven men got out. Two were subsequently caught—one of whom was Capt. Sam. Taylor, a gallant young officer, about twenty-two years of age, and a nephew of the renowned "Old Zack." He is now a prisoner at Fort Delaware.

[26] Captain Thomas W. Harris, a native of Oglethorpe, Georgia, was captured May 12, 1864 at Spotsylvania County, Virginia following the Battle of the Wilderness. He would later become part of a group of Confederate prisoners taken to Morris Island, South Carolina, at the entrance to Charleston Harbor to serve as human shields in retaliation to the Confederates having placed fifty Union officers in the city of Charleston, South Carolina, to serve as human shields to prevent shelling of the city. The group of soldiers, including Captain Harris, would be known throughout the Confederacy as "the immortal 600."

[27] Handy Diary: Friday, May 20, 1864: It has been ten months, to-day, since my arrest. I have had many trying, anxious moments during this time, and I have suffered much, both in body and mind; but I thank God, I was ever brought to Fort Delaware. That His providence has had to do with it, I cannot

doubt. A field of usefulness has been opened to me, more important, perhaps, than I could have occupied elsewhere. How I have tried to cultivate it, He knows, and eternity can only reveal with what result.

The meeting at half-past ten o'clock was well attended, both by church members and inquirers. Lieutenants H—s, H—e, M—y, and T—t have each expressed a hope in Christ. Lieut. B—l also thinks, he has experienced the great change, but hesitates about a present open profession. Have conversed freely with all these young men, and tried to lead them in the paths of righteousness.

Had a pleasant interview with Col. Davidson, of North Carolina. He is a large, fine looking man, and an officer in the 7th regiment. He comes from Charlotte, and is a blood-relation of the Brevards, whose history is so intimately associated with the Mecklinburg Declaration. He tells me that he has lost a brother in battle, and the he has furnished the Historical Society of North Carolina with an account of his life and death.

I have procured a number of small hymn-books (Union Prayer-meeting) from Chaplain Way, for the use of our meetings, and have distributed them to-day, much to the delights of the brethren, and especially of those who are prominent in keeping up the services.

A bar-room is about to be opened by the sutler, at which liquor will be sold by the drink, instead of the bottle, as heretofore. How strangely inconsistent are these Yankees! They advertise liquor as contraband article; sell it by the quantity, or small, as they can venture to do it; wink at the drunkenness, provided it does not become public; and then punish the first demonstration of it on the part of prisoners—although they are frequently intoxicated themselves, and that with perfect impunity.

The Masonic Fraternity are holding regular meetings in a division, which is allowed them for the purpose. I understand, that about one hundred persons are assembling in this capacity. A Lyceum has also been organized, which meets once a week.

A private prayer-meeting has been established, the object of which is, to pray for growth in grace, and for guidance in regard to the best modes of operating for God's glory, and the regard of souls whilst in prison. At present the number is restricted to such persons, as are willing to engage with one another to enter upon the work before them.

morning at 10 o'clock and proved a great blessing especially to backsliders who were anxious to renew their vows to their Lord. Here they were met by the ministers and brethren and freely conversed with each other in regard to their true moral conditions. The exercise at these meetings usually consisted of singing, prayer, reading the scriptures and religious conversation. Many who had been long luke warm in the service of his Master will thank God in all time to come that they attended the inquiry meeting at Fort Delaware. On this also was organized a noonday prayer meeting. The primary object of this meeting was to invoke God's blessing upon the church for strengthening Christians for their growth in grace and an increase in faith, that they might be the better instruments in the hands of God for doing good. But four persons were present at this organization. Capt. Shane at whose suggestion it

---

The good weather of has dried up the mud and water in "the pen," and many of the young men amuse themselves with various athletic sports, of which Prisoners' Base seems to be the most popular. These sports can the more readily be carried on just now, in consequence of the removal of the guard from the interior—a strange thing, nevertheless, as but a few days have elapsed, since a sentinel shot at an officer for simple crossing the middle walk. Now the whole yard is free, and no sentinel is posted, except on the outside. Why could this not have been done before?—and why should such unreasonable restraints have been imposed at the first?

The evening services were conducted by Capt. Samford, who addressed a full house, on the subjects of thanksgiving, and vows. His remarks were good, and reciecved, I think, with profit.

was instituted being one of the number. But at each succeeding meeting the number gradually increased until all the active members of the church were regular attendants. The exercises of these meetings were the same as those of the meeting of inquire; singing, prayer reading, scriptures and religious experience. On June the 25th [1864][28], the time of the meeting was changed to morning instead of

---

[28] **Handy Diary: Saturday, June 25, 1864: Moved into 34, and ensconced myself in the south-east corner, near the preaching stand, at the end of the room. I have a window, which looks out upon the tents and buildings on the side of the Island next the Jersey shore. I have fixed up a sort of extempore writing shelf, and have a good shelf also for by books; but my head sweeps the white-washed ceiling, constituting the floor of the tier above, and any quantity of dust is falling continually. I have already had an impudent challenge from the outside sentinel, who has ordered me to keep on the inside of my slatted window. The order was unnecessary, for I have done no more than peep out, and that without showing any one of my extremities on his side of the dividing wall.**

A new arrangement has been adopted, to-day, in regard to our entrance to meals, by which crowds of prisoners are detained, half an hour or more, standing in the hot sun, waiting their turns—each man being admitted slowly, and by single file, through a narrow opening to the table. This is an imposition which must go very hard with some of us, if we continue to visit the hall, Were it not for the bread, I would never go to the table—for the coarse beef and nasty soup are really disgusting to my too delicate palate.
About six hundred and fifty men were introduced into the barracks in the course of the afternoon, crowding every "she-bang" very nearly to its utmost capacity. In 34 we have upwards of ninety men, although the division is one of the shortest in the entire range. Among the new-comers I find Capt. H. A. Allen and Lieut—Shannon, of the "Old Dominion Guards," Portsmouth.
Spent much of the day in conversing with the late converts, chiefly on the subject of the ordinances. Had special talks with Maj. A. R—, Capts. W. H. G— and F. H. McC—, and Lieuts. E. L. B— and E. A. S—, who have had troubles, on the subject of baptism. A majority of them seem, now, to be entirely relieved, and will be admitted to this seal of the covenant, on to-morrow.

noon. On May the 26th [1864] [29] in the evening another prayer meeting was organized Capt. G.W. Moore, W.R. White and W.C. Shane. These brethren designed their meetings to be private. They

---

Our meeting for the admission of members was deeply interesting. Thirty officers, mostly young men; gave full and explicit statements, in regard to their past lives, and the evidence of their new condition. I have never heard anything more satisfactory, in all my ministry, of twenty-five years. Without exception, every man could give good "reason for the hope that is in him," and apparently, "With meekness and fear." All seem to be truly penitent sinners, trusting only in the merits of a crucified Redeemer; earnestly desiring newness of life; with heartfelt impression of utter inability to accomplish any good work, without the gracious aid of the Spirit. The meeting continued nearly three hours, with unfailing interest to the last.

Had a long talk, after night, in the open air, with Capt. H—about the call, and qualifications necessary to the work of the ministry. His mind has been greatly troubled on this subject; and I was glad to leave him much encouraged, and I hope entirely relieved, as to the obligations in his own case. My window gives me an opportunity of seeing something of the movements outside of "the pen." Great numbers of privates have been hard at work, all day—many of them bare-footed, and all of them looking shabby, and dirty enough—toiling away at the old business of carrying boards. I have no doubt the exercise is good for them; and they get an additional ration; but it is really unpleasant to see the poor fellows driven about by Yankee guards, often abused, and always meekly submitting to every indignity. They have accomplished a vast amount of work during the year; and it is to them that the Yankees are indebted for nearly all the improvements on the island.

[29]   [Thursday, May 26, 1864] Damp and rainy; and the floor of the division covered in mud and water.

Increased attendance at the inquiry meeting. Capt R_____s still in the dark.

Conference meeting as usual, at 12 M. Addressed by Capt. Gordon, Lieut. Bullock, and myself.

Preached at night from Rom. Xiii. 11: "Now it is high time to awake out of sleep." Three persons ask for prayers of the church.

47

remained in the chapel after the dismissal of regular prayer meetings to pray and for each other.

The several evening they kept their meeting strictly secret, but soon others were admitted until their meeting numbered 10 or 12 brethren. These meeting were kept up as long as a place of meeting could be obtained. Two or three mourners would remain each night with these brethren to be prayed for. They often remained in secret communion with their God until the night was far spent. And it was not infrequently the case that mourners heavily laden with sin came forth from these meeting new creatures in Christ Jesus. It was not long after this meeting was established until another prayer meeting was organized at the suggestion of Dr. Handy. It was instituted exclusively for young converts whom there were at this time about twenty. These meeting were conducted by the young brethren alternately; none others attending. The exercises being the same as those of the inquiry meeting. The revival was not in full progress. Dr. Handy's daily labors commencing on the 13th Capt. Harris arrived on the 19th accompanied by a large number of energetic Christians and all uniting their efforts to advance the Kingdom of Christ. The good cause received additional strength and gradually increased until great good was accomplished. One interesting feature of this revival was the absence of excitement common on such occasions. Convictions were silent and deep, and conversions calm and thorough. Christians at all times were fervent in the spirit serving the Lord. Brethren of all denominations assisted in the exercises. No party lines were drawn or known but all labored together cheerfully in the Lord's vineyard and God vouchsafed his spirit in answer to the petitions of his servants and its blest influence was felt by both saint and sinner. Thursday June 9th [1864] was set apart as a day of fasting, humiliation and prayer for the outpouring of God's Holy Spirit on the whole island and to invoke the mercies and blessing of God upon our bleeding Country the Confederate States of America. This day was observed as such by all Christians and during the day prayers were continually ascending from more than a hundred hearts to a throne of grace fro the sinful comrades and desolated country. These prayers were abundantly answered in the conversion of sinners and the building up of Christians. June 25th [1864][30] was a day appointed for the examination of applicants for

---

[30] **Handy Diary: Saturday, June 25, 1864: Moved into 34, and ensconced myself in the south-east corner, near the preaching stand, at the end of the room. I have a window, which looks out upon the tents and buildings on the side of the Island next the Jersey shore. I have fixed up a sort of extempore writing shelf, and have a good shelf also for by books; but my head sweeps the white-washed ceiling, constituting the floor of the tier above, and any quantity of dust is falling continually. I have already had an impudent challenge from the outside sentinel, who has ordered me to keep on the inside of my slatted window. The order was unnecessary, for I have done no more than peep out, and that without showing any one of my extremities on his side of the dividing wall.**

A new arrangement has been adopted, to-day, in regard to our entrance to meals, by which crowds of prisoners are detained, half an hour or more, standing in the hot sun, waiting their turns—each man being admitted slowly,

admission into the Church at large by Dr. Handy, Capt. Samford and Capt. Harris. But the day prior to this we were notified by the

---

and by single file, through a narrow opening to the table. This is an imposition which must go very hard with some of us, if we continue to visit the hall, Were it not for the bread, I would never go to the table—for the coarse beef and nasty soup are really disgusting to my too delicate palate.

About six hundred and fifty men were introduced into the barracks in the course of the afternoon, crowding every "she-bang" very nearly to its utmost capacity. In 34 we have upwards of ninety men, although the division is one of the shortest in the entire range. Among the new-comers I find Capt. H. A. Allen and Lieut—Shannon, of the "Old Dominion Guards," Portsmouth.

Spent much of the day in conversing with the late converts, chiefly on the subject of the ordinances. Had special talks with Maj. A. R—, Capts. W. H. G— and F. H. McC—, and Lieuts. E. L. B— and E. A. S—, who have had troubles, on the subject of baptism. A majority of them seem, now, to be entirely relieved, and will be admitted to this seal of the covenant, on to-morrow.

Our meeting for the admission of members was deeply interesting. Thirty officers, mostly young men; gave full and explicit statements, in regard to their past lives, and the evidence of their new condition. I have never heard anything more satisfactory, in all my ministry, of twenty-five years. Without exception, every man could give good "reason for the hope that is in him," and apparently, "With meekness and fear." All seem to be truly penitent sinners, trusting only in the merits of a crucified Redeemer; earnestly desiring newness of life; with heartfelt impression of utter inability to accomplish any good work, without the gracious aid of the Spirit. The meeting continued nearly three hours, with unfailing interest to the last.

Had a long talk, after night, in the open air, with Capt. H—about the call, and qualifications necessary to the work of the ministry. His mind has been greatly troubled on this subject; and I was glad to leave him much encouraged, and I hope entirely relieved, as to the obligations in his own case.

My window gives me an opportunity of seeing something of the movements outside of "the pen." Great numbers of privates have been hard at work, all day—many of them bare-footed, and all of them looking shabby, and dirty enough—toiling away at the old business of carrying boards. I have no doubt the exercise is good for them; and they get an additional ration; but it is really unpleasant to see the poor fellows driven about by Yankee guards, often abused, and always meekly submitting to every indignity. They have accomplished a vast amount of work during the year; and it is to them that the Yankees are indebted for nearly all the improvements on the island.

authorities that six hundred prisoners of war from Ft. Lookout, Md. be here and the room then used for a chapel must be given up. This was the only interruption of our meeting since the 10th of May [1864][31] and plans were soon put on foot to remedy this. The

---

[31] **Handy Diary: Tuesday, May 10, 1864: We have had several days of unusually fine weather. The Delaware river has been as smooth as glass— while vessels have appeared as usual, in every direction.**

Visited the officers' quarters, and found the political prisoners located in the vicinity of the west gate, next door to the sutler, who has established himself in "the pen," near the bank. Regretted to notice several of the Politicals but just recovering from a heavy "drunk," and was informed that a number of officers had joined with them in the spree. Altogether, they have a had a "high old time." Among the first whom I discovered in a state of intoxication, was one in whom I felt special interest, and who promised me weeks ago, never to touch the poison again. How often it is that a "man resolves, and resolves, and yet does the same."

The awakening continues. A number of persons have, among whom are Capt. H. H. M—, and Lieuts. J. H—, J. M—, and R. T—, with all of whom I have had free conversations, and find them not far from the Kingdom of Heaven. I have advised them according to their several phases of experience, and pray God to lead them in the way of all truth.

The two pens, occupied severally by officers and privates, are separated by fences, which stand about fifteen or twenty feet apart. These fences are guarded by sentinels, who perambulate an elevated platform, from which they may overlook the two enclosures. It requires considerable dexterity to elude the watchful of the rough "blue coats," who are there night and day. The cunning "Rebs" have found an expedient, in every pebble of suitable weight to secure the necessary impetus for communication across the parapet. Notes are constantly falling into the area on the officers' side, complaining of hard usage by the Yankee authorities, and asking help or redress from the Confederate leaders. To-day, one of the little carrier pigeons brought the following to Gen. Vance:

number of conversions up to this time was about thirty and others
still inquiring the way to Jesus. And to prevent a complete cessation

---

Soldiers' Quarters,
Fort Del., *April 28th, 1864.*

To Gen. Robert B. Vance,
      Or any other Rebel officer:
Prompted by the gnawing of hunger, I am emboldened to make this appeal to you; hoping that being informed of our sufferings, you can and will appeal to the Commanding General in our behalf, and if possible have our rations increased.

For breakfast we get one-fifth of a loaf of bread, and from four to six ounces of meat—fresh or salt beef, or both—and a pint of very inferior coffee. For dinner we get the same amount of bread and meat—Sunday and Wednesday excepted—when, instead of meat, we get two or three potatoes, and a cup of bean or rice soup. As to supper, we have none.
Whether the rations are allowed us by the authorities and wasted by the cooks, I cannot say, as I do not know. But one thing is certain, we are suffering.

                        Respectfully,
                        A Hungry Rebel

The note was handed to Gen. Vance, who, feeling it to be his duty to do so, presented it to Gen. Schœpf. The immediate reply was: "Say to them, for their consolation—*the rations are to be reduced.*"

The authorities are "shutting down" upon the prisoners, in every part of the island. Officers and privates are, alike, subject to the rigors of this change. Rations are to be reduced; paroles are to be restricted; and there are strong indications of an entirely new order of things. A notice has been stuck up in the hall, in regard to a more systematic, and regular inspection of the rooms; and an order has been issued, restricting prisoners of war on parole, to very circumscribed limits, and disallowing all intercourse between them and the officers at the barracks.

Unfavorable news by the "grape vine!" The Yankees are encouraged!

Heard a musket fire, and noticed a great running towards the barracks. What is the matter?

of religious exercises, seventy brethren agreed to occupy a division and permit the regular daily exercises to be conducted in their division and thus religious worship was kept up as before after a slight interruption. In the meantime, the examination of the young converts was not lost sight of. But at the time appointed, a committee composed of Dr. Handy, Capt. Samford, Capt. Harris, Capt. Tracy, Capt. Eastin and Maj. Bullock, these brethren representing the different churches, assembled and examined the applicants. This examination was not conducted according [to] the established form of any particular church, but each member of the committee was expected to ask such questions as he thought necessary until all were satisfied when the vote was taken for the admission or rejection of the brethren. There was thirty brethren examined and all decided by the committee to be fit subjects for church membership, and were so reported by the committee the day following. As was anticipated six hundred officers prisoners of war arrived here from Ft. Lookout[32] today the 25th June [1864][33]. Of this

---

[32] Point Lookout POW Camp was established along the southern tip of Maryland following the Battle of Gettysburg (July 1-3, 1863) to accommodate the scores of captured Confederate soldiers. It was in operation from August 1863 until June 1865. The camp was known for its unsanitary conditions with over 14,000 Confederate soldiers dying during their incarceration.

[33] **Handy Diary: Saturday, June 25, 1864: Moved into 34, and ensconced myself in the south-east corner, near the preaching stand, at the end of the room. I have a window, which looks out upon the tents and buildings on the side of the Island next the Jersey shore. I have fixed up a sort of extempore writing shelf, and have a good shelf also for by books; but my head sweeps**

the white-washed ceiling, constituting the floor of the tier above, and any quantity of dust is falling continually. I have already had an impudent challenge from the outside sentinel, who has ordered me to keep on the inside of my slatted window. The order was unnecessary, for I have done no more than peep out, and that without showing any one of my extremities on his side of the dividing wall.

A new arrangement has been adopted, to-day, in regard to our entrance to meals, by which crowds of prisoners are detained, half an hour or more, standing in the hot sun, waiting their turns—each man being admitted slowly, and by single file, through a narrow opening to the table. This is an imposition which must go very hard with some of us, if we continue to visit the hall, Were it not for the bread, I would never go to the table—for the coarse beef and nasty soup are really disgusting to my too delicate palate.

About six hundred and fifty men were introduced into the barracks in the course of the afternoon, crowding every "she-bang" very nearly to its utmost capacity. In 34 we have upwards of ninety men, although the division is one of the shortest in the entire range. Among the new-comers I find Capt. H. A. Allen and Lieut—Shannon, of the "Old Dominion Guards," Portsmouth.

Spent much of the day in conversing with the late converts, chiefly on the subject of the ordinances. Had special talks with Maj. A. R—, Capts. W. H. G— and F. H. McC—, and Lieuts. E. L. B— and E. A. S—, who have had troubles, on the subject of baptism. A majority of them seem, now, to be entirely relieved, and will be admitted to this seal of the covenant, on to-morrow.

Our meeting for the admission of members was deeply interesting. Thirty officers, mostly young men; gave full and explicit statements, in regard to their past lives, and the evidence of their new condition. I have never heard anything more satisfactory, in all my ministry, of twenty-five years. Without exception, every man could give good "reason for the hope that is in him," and apparently, "With meekness and fear." All seem to be truly penitent sinners, trusting only in the merits of a crucified Redeemer; earnestly desiring newness of life; with heartfelt impression of utter inability to accomplish any good work, without the gracious aid of the Spirit. The meeting continued nearly three hours, with unfailing interest to the last.

Had a long talk, after night, in the open air, with Capt. H—about the call, and qualifications necessary to the work of the ministry. His mind has been greatly troubled on this subject; and I was glad to leave him much encouraged, and I hope entirely relieved, as to the obligations in his own case. My window gives me an opportunity of seeing something of the movements outside of "the pen." Great numbers of privates have been hard at work, all

large accession of prisoners there was two ministers, Lieut. D.P. Thomas of Tenn. And Lt. G.W. Carter of Ark. and a large number of professors of Christianity. Some of them had been confined before their removal to Ft. Lookout at Johnson's Island and had there participated in a glorious revival of religion. And while at Ft. Lookout, their labors had been kept up to some extent. They entered heartly [sic] into the work with us and labored for the good of souls. The second communion, Sunday, June 26th [1864][34] will be long

---

day—many of them bare-footed, and all of them looking shabby, and dirty enough—toiling away at the old business of carrying boards. I have no doubt the exercise is good for them; and they get an additional ration; but it is really unpleasant to see the poor fellows driven about by Yankee guards, often abused, and always meekly submitting to every indignity. They have accomplished a vast amount of work during the year; and it is to them that the Yankees are indebted for nearly all the improvements on the island.

[34] Handy Diary: Sunday, June 26, 1864: This has been one of the most remarkable Sabbaths of my life. In some respects it has been the most interesting; and certainly the most promising of important results. In the morning, I preached to the largest congregation which has yet assembled for worship, in "the pen." The body of the room; every bunk of the three tiers; every nook, and corner—all, were stowed full, and to their utmost capacity, with attentive, and devout hearers. The subject of my discourse was, *The nature and importance of a public confession of Christ,* from the text Heb. Iii. 1: "*Our profession."* With many before me, to whom the subject was specifically applicable; and with the expectation that a score and a half of them would, in the afternoon, for the first time, appear before the world, bearing the badge of the Cross, I felt animated, and earnest in the effort to instruct them aright.

In the afternoon, the Bible class was suspended, in consequence of the arrangements for the Supper. Intending to hold the services in the open air, we were discouraged, just about the hour for convening, be the appearance of a storm. The wind blew considerably; dark clouds floated in the sky; and anon, a few heavy drops of rain descended. We waited anxiously, and in doubt. Presently all apprehension was at an end. The storm subsided; and the bright sun beamed cheerfully upon the prison campus.

In a few moments, a long rough table was placed near the division fence. A few benches were adjusted for the benefit of such of the communicants as might prefer to kneel; and, then, the crowd arranged themselves on the ground, right and left, as far as the voice could be well heard, with a good congregation, also, in front. The preliminary services were conducted, in the usual manner. After reading Matthew's account of the crucifixion, and the words of the institution by the Apostle to the Gentiles—the nature of the ordinance was expounded; believers were encouraged, and the wicked and impenitent warned to abstain from an act, which must only bring condemnation upon their souls.

All those who were examined, on yesterday, now came forward, as their names were called, and publicly answered affirmatively, to a series of questions involving the first principles of the Gospel. The body of Christians then arose, acknowledging them as members of the same communion with themselves. Eight persons were baptized, by sprinkling, as they severally stood around the long table, which—without premeditation—I ascended, for greater convenience; and by solemnity, to apply the holy seal, in full observation of the large assembly. The persons baptized were Capts. W. F Gordon, Jr., G. W. Kurtz, and Lieuts. Jasper Horne, F. M. Noble, E. Lee Bell, Francis Holmes, John Paul, and F. M. McCuistion—some of whom had been troubled on the subject, but were now satisfied, both as to the nature and method of the sacrament.

In consequence of having but two glasses, one of them much smaller than the other, we were considerably interrupted in serving the wine. The persons engaged in the distribution of the elements were Capts. A. M. Samford, and Thomas W. Harris, Methodist preachers; Capt. C. L. Bennett, of the Christian Church; and Lieut. John. C. Allen, Presbyterian, and Ruling Elder. This arrangement was the best that could be effected in the spirit of brotherly love, and with a view to union and harmony. A large majority of the communicants were seated on the ground, whilst many kneeled at the benches provided for the purpose. If it were ever possible, on this earth, for a great concourse of Christians, of different names, to assemble "with one heart and one mind," that assemblage convened to-day. Truly our hearts were melted together in love. There was no word of opposition; no jar; aye—may I not say?—no thought of separation in any heart. Oh, how did our gushing souls well up in the spirit of that gracious, happy song:

remembered by many of us. Dr. Handy [gave] an elegant sermon from the text our profession "in the morning."

"Let party names no more
The Christian world o'erspread:
Gentile and Jew, and bond and free.
Are one in Christ in their Head

"Among the saints on earth,
Let mutual love be found,
Heirs of the same inheritance,
With mutual blessings crown'd.

"Thus will the Church below,
Resemble that above,
Where streams of pleasure ever flow,
And every heart is love."

Four of the young men who joined the church, to-day, are sons of ministers of the Gospel.

Being unaccustomed to speak in the open air, felt much fatigued after the services, and my lungs were sore. Had the impression that my remarks lacked force, and unction; and as the winds cut off my words, occasioning a constant strain of the voice, I felt annoyed, and had considerable difficulty in retaining a proper current of thought. It was nevertheless a happy day; and I do believe, it will long be remembered by the hundreds who witnessed its solemn and impressive scenes.

We were marshaled into meals, to-day, by divisions—a better plan than heretofore, requiring less time, and securing to each man his own ration.
Four Lieutenants were taken to the Fort, this evening, and placed in close confinement. The cause unknown.

The discourse was an earnest admonition for all believers to attach themselves to some one of the evangelical churches, and take a decided stand on the Lord's side. Showing the church to be the proper place and safest place for believers. At the conclusion of the morning services it was announced that the Lord's supper would be administrated in the evening at 3 o'clock. Accordingly at the time appointed a large majority of prisoners in the barracks assembled in the open air to witness or participate in the Lord's suffering and death. Dr. Handy who might be called very appropriately the Chaplain for the Confederate Officers at Fort Delaware conducted the meeting. After the usual preliminary exercises and a few brief remarks explaninatory [sic] of the nature design and importance of the Holy institution about to be observed. He preceded to receive publically in the Church at large the converts who had been examined by the committee on the day before. These as their names were called came forward and arranged themselves around the alter where the usual questions were propounded and answered. After which they were by unanimous vote received into full fellowship. The following is a list of names rank and residences those thus received: W.T. Aud, Political Prisoner, Poolesville, Maryland, A.H. Baily, Lieut 14th Virginia Cavalry, T.W. Bullitt, Lieut 2nd Kentucky Cavalry, Louisville, Kentucky, J.B. Baker, Lieut 3rd Kentucky Cavalry, Plattsburg, Maryland, E.L. Bell, Lieut 10th Virginia, Surney, Virginia, J.F. Caldwell, Lieut 8th Missouri Cavalry, Dallas,

Missouri, J.F. Davis, Lieut 14th Georgia, Jackson, Georgia, A.E. Edgar, Captain 29th Virginia, Lewisburg, Virginia, J.H. Guthrie, Lieut 10th Virginia Cavalry, Pankeyville, Alabama, W.F. Gorden, Capt. Jinkins Cavalry, Clarksburg, Virginia, F. Holmes, Lieut 29th Mississippi, Hornlake, Mississippi, Jasper Horne, Lieut 9th Tennessee, Columbus, Tennessee, W.L. Hunter, Lieut 43rd Virginia, Waynesboro, Virginia, H.L.W. Johnson, Capt. 12th Arkansas, Okelona, Arkansas, G.W. Kurtz, Capt. 5th Virginia, Winchester, Virginia, J.F. Lytton, Captain 5th Virginia, Long Glade, Virginia, J.L. Mays, Lieut. 19th Arkansas, Fayetteville, Arkansas, W.H. Morris, Lieut 2nd Kentucky Cavalry, Lexington, Kentucky, J.T. Mackey, Lieut 48th Tennessee, Columbia, Tennessee, F.H. McChristine, Lieut. Huntsville, Arkansas, H.M. Middleton, Captain 39th Georgia, Somerville, Georgia, F.M. Noble, Lieut. 3rd Texas, Flora, Texas, John Paul, Lieut. 1st Virginia Cavalry, W.F. Robbins, Captain 28th Alabama, H. Reed, Major, Mississippi Cavalry, B.E. Roberts, Captain, Monticello, Kentucky, E.A. Street, Lieut 14th Tennessee, Ripley, Mississippi, R. Tollant, Lieut Arkansas Battalion, Hot Springs, Arkansas, T.E. Bookter, Captain Mississippi Cavalry, Starkville, Mississipi. The following number of the above brethren were then Baptised [sic] by Dr. Handy: Captain W.F. Gordon of Virginia, F.H. McChristian of Arkansas, Lieut Jasper Horne of Tennessee, E.L. Bell of Virginia, F.M. Noble of Texas, John Paul of Virginia.

After the administration of the ordinance of Baptism, the elements representing the broken body and shed blood of our Lord and Savior, Jesus Christ, were placed on the table and those who believed on [H]is name gathered around the board. Here was truly an interesting scene and one that Angels delighted to witness. The communicates were more than two hundred in number, and there not being seats for all. They arranged themselves promiscuously around the sacred board on the ground. The audience gathered around and in silence surveyed the scene. The four ministers, Dr. Handy, Captain Samford, Captain Harris, and Lieut Thomas stood [to] one side of the table and those just Baptized on the other. The bread was broken by our venerable brother Dr. Handy. And was given to the disciples with that solemn injuction [sic]. "Take eat this is my body" and he took the cup and gave thanks and gave it to them saying drink ye all of it. For this is my blood of the New Testament which is shed for the remission of sins. For so often as you eat this bread and drink this cup ye do show the Lord's death till he come. Not a sound was heard save the low soft read [?] of those who bore the sacred elements to their brethren. A hymn ws sung and the impressive service was over, and that band of disciples separated, never to meet again perhaps under similar circumstances, they had met that day many of them for the first time and had drank of the same cup and mingles their voices in supplication to a throne of grace. They parted and when shall they all commune with their GOD together again. They had been thrown togather [sic] and might soon be torn asunder never to meet again until gathered around the Throne of Him who [who] is judge quick and dead. Some had that day for the first time tasted the broken body and shed blood of their Saviour [sic], and rejoiced in the hope of Heaven. On the day following certificates of Church membership were given to those who had been admitted to full fellowship on the day before. The design the certificates as the commendation of the brethren to all Christian Churches whenever and where ever presented and as a special recommendation to any particular Church the brother might wish to connect himself with.

[END OF DIARY]

Appendix A

Biographical Sketch of
1st Lieutenant James Vance Walker

James Vance Walker was born January 14, 1838 in Bradley County, Tennessee, the eldest of ten children of William Houston Walker and Polly Poe. While a young man, the Walker family moved to nearby McMinn County, Tennessee, where Walker worked on the family farm.

At the outbreak of the Civil War, the Walker family was divided with James Vance and his father, William Houston, enlisting in the Confederate cause while his uncle, Daniel Walker, remained true to the Union.

James Vance enlisted into Confederate service at Calhoun (McMinn County), Tennessee on May 3, 1861. Following his enlistment, he and the other new Confederate recruits left Calhoun on May 7,1861 bound for Knoxville, Tennessee. From there they were sent by rail to Lynchburg, Virginia where James Vance was mustered into Confederate service on June 2, 1861 as a Sargent in Company "G" of the Third Tennessee Confederate Infantry.[35] The unit was initially placed under command of Colonel Ambrose Hill along with the Tenth Virginia infantry. Walker first saw action on June 19, 1861 at the Battle of New Creek, Virginia.

On June 21, 1861, Walker and the Third Tennessee, who were assigned to the Confederate Division under command of General Edmund Kirby Smith, were dispatched to Manasssas, Virginia where they participated in the Battle of Bull Run.

Following the Battle of Bull Run, the Third Tennessee was transferred to the command of Brigadier General Arnold Elzey participating in the Battles of Morgan and Scott County, Tennessee

---

[35] There were actually two Third Tennessee Infantry units. James Vance Walker's unit was initially commanded by Colonel John C. Vaughn and later by Colonel Newton Lillard. This unit is generally referred to as "Vaughn's Brigade" or "Lillard's Infantry."

[March 28, 1862], Battle of Tazewell, Tennessee [August 6, 1862] and the Battle of Perryville, Kentucky [October 8, 1862].

On May 15, 1862, Walker was elected 1st Lieutenant and promoted to commander of Company "G."

In December 1862, the regiment was ordered to Vicksburg, Mississippi where it would form the rear guard of Lt. General John C. Pemberton's Army on their May 1863 march to Raymond, Mississippi. As part of the Vicksburg Campaign, Walker participated in the Battle of Champion Hill, Mississippi on May 16, 1863 and Big Black River, Mississippi on May 17, 1863. Following those battles, the Confederates retreated to the trenches at Vicksburg where it was active during the siege by Federal troops until the surrender of Confederate forces on July 4, 1863.

Following the surrender of the Confederate army and his parole, Walker returned to Tennessee where the Third Tennessee was reformed. On February 1, 1864, Walker was captured in Murray County, Georgia by bushwhackers. He was initially sent to the Union prison camp at Camp Chase, Ohio, before being transferred to Fort Delaware officer's prison where he remained for the duration of the war, being released on June 17, 1865 after signing an oath of allegiance to the United States.

Following the war's end, Walker returned to McMinn County, Tennessee, where he operated a grist mill on Spring Creek. He was active in Confederate veteran affairs after the war and attended several veteran reunions. He was also active in his church, the Spring Creek Methodist Church, where he served as a Deacon. He married Keziah Ann Morgan and had seven daughters and three sons. James Vance Walker died of pneumonia on April 8, 1923 and is buried in Spring Creek Cemetery in Calhoun, Tennessee

James Vance Walker

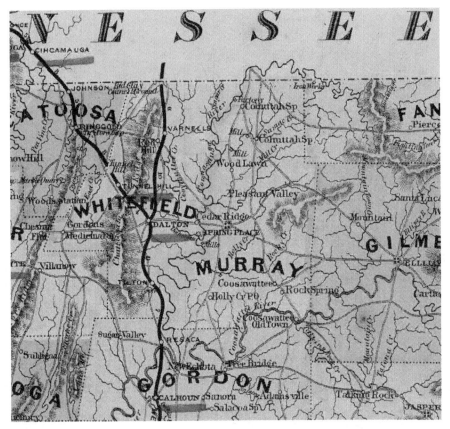

1864 map of Murray County, Georgia. It was here that bushwhackers captured James Vance Walker on February 1, 1864 while on a mission to recruit additional soldiers for his unit, the Third Tennessee Confederate Infantry (Vaughn's).

[Source: Lloyd's Topographical Map of Georgia, 1864]

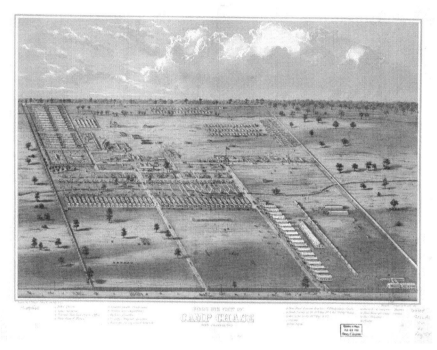

Camp Chase Military Prison near Columbus, Ohio. It was here that James Vance Walker was initially taken following his capture in February of 1864. Walker would remain at Camp Chase only a short time before being transported to Fort Delaware Military Prison in Delaware where he would remain for the duration of the war.

[Source: Library of Congress G4084.C6:2C3A3 186- .R8]

Appendix B

Biographical Sketch of
Reverend Isaac W.K. Handy

Isaac William Ker Handy was born December 14, 1815 in Washington D.C., the eldest son of James Henry Handy (1789-1832) and Maria Ann Pitts Gillis (1794-1839). Education was stressed at an early age with Handy being tutored by various teachers, among them Salmon P. Chase, Secretary of the Treasury under President Abraham Lincoln and later, Chief Justice of the United States Supreme Court. After briefly attending the academy at Charlotte Hall, Maryland, Handy would graduate from Jefferson College, in Washington, Pennsylvania, in 1834.

Handy expressed a provision of faith at an early age; entering the Princeton Theological Seminary in November of 1835. The Presbytery of the District of Columbia licensed him on April 3, 1838. He was ordained November 22, 1838 and installed the same day as pastor of three churches (Buckingham, Blackwater and Laurel) where he served until October 11, 1844.

Following his stint at the three churches, Handy moved westward, settling in Warsaw, Missouri, where he served for three years before returning east, accepting the pastorship of two churches, at Odessa and Port Penn, where he served for two years. Handy shifted localities once again in 1853 when he became a missionary for the eastern peninsula of Maryland.

On April 16, 1857, Handy accepted and was installed as pastor of the church at Portsmouth, Virginia. It was during the period at Portsmouth that controversy landed him in trouble – serious trouble. At the onset of the Civil War, the Presbyterian Church took the position opposing slavery. Handy, one of the leaders of the southern branch of the Presbyterian Church favored Secession. He was outspoken in his beliefs, even expressing his secessionist views in the north while visiting relatives. It was on one such visit he was detained by northern authorities for his "radical opinions" and taken to the military prison at Fort Delaware, Delaware. Here he remained for fifteen months, where he spent his time ministering to the Confederate Officers imprisoned in the fort. During his time as a political prisoner, Handy maintained a daily diary, which he published in 1874 under the title "*United States Bonds or Duress by Federal Authority: A Journal of Current Events During Impisonment of Fifteen Months, at Fort Delaware*."

Following his release from Fort Delaware, Handy remained at the church in Portsmouth, Virginia until August 8, 1865 when he left to accept the pastorship at churches in Orange Court House and Gordonsville, Virginia, where he remained until 1870. On May 13, 1870, Handy was installed as Pastor of the Presbyterian Church in Augusta, Virginia, and a position he held until his death on June 14, 1878. He was buried at the Augusta Stone Presbyterian Church cemetery in Fort Defiance, Virginia.

Handy was married three times: (1) Mary Jane Rozelle (1821-1848) whom he married in 1839. (2) Sara Selby Martin (---- - 1853) whom he married in 1850 and (3) Rebecca Dilworth (1825-1913) whom he married in 1855.

Handy fathered eleven children; five with Mary Rozelle, one with Sara Martin and five with Rebecca Dilworth. A large number of descendants survive today.

Dr. Isaac W.K. Handy

[Source: Fort Delaware Historical Society]

Reverend Isaac Handy (center, wearing civilian clothing), surrounded by Confederate officers at Fort Delaware Federal Prison, April 1864.

[Source: Fort Delaware Historical Society]

Appendix C

The History of Fort Delaware

The area now known as Fort Delaware had its roots back to 1794 when the property was surveyed by Pierre Charles L'Enfant who referred to the site as "pip ash" and was impressed with its defensive possibilities. L'Enfant is most often remembered for his designing the layout of the city of Washington D.C.

During the War of 1812, efforts were made to fortify the site, although with the exception of a seawall and some dykes, little evidence remains of any serious construction.

The federal government decided upon a star fort design, with construction of what would become Fort Delaware beginning December 8, 1817. However, the swampy area the fort was built upon would plague construction, and it would not be until 1825 when the area was occupied by the military, with the fourth US Artillery housed there under command of Major Alexander Fanning.

During the Civil War, the fort was converted from a defensive structure to one used to house some of the tens of thousands of Confederate prisoners being captured throughout the battlefields of the south. Every available space was utilized to house the Confederate prisoners. During 1862 and 1863, additional construction was done to add barracks for the ever increasing number of prisoners. In addition to the barracks, a large hospital was built on the site to deal with the constant threat of disease within the fort.

By 1863 the fort held more than 11,000 prisoners on the island. This would grow to over 30,000 by war's end.

In the years following its use as a Civil War fort, the island was ravaged by nature with a hurricane in 1878 and tornado in 1885 destroying much of the civil war era construction.

Following the Civil War, the site was again occupied by the US military, placing an artillery unit to help safeguard again foreign aggression. This was amplified during both the Spanish-American War and the World War I where 12-inch guns helped protect the area.

Following the attack on Pearl Harbor in 1941, the fort was again called into action with elements of the US Artillery assigned to the island.

In 1947, the state of Delaware acquired the site from the United States who had deemed it surplus property.

The Fort Delaware Society was created in 1950 in an effort to help preserve the history of the island. The society has done an outstanding job at not only interpretation but of preserving the history of the site for future generations.

Appendix D

Military Service Record
of
James Vance Walker
1st Lieutenant, Company G
Third Tennessee Confederate Infantry
(Vaughn's Brigade)

(Image Quality Poor)

Walker, James V.

Co. G , 3 (Lillard's)
Tennessee Mounted Infantry.

Formerly 3 Tenn. Inf.
Reg't mounted about Jan. 1, '64.

(Confederate.)

Sergeant Lieutenant

CARD NUMBERS.

1	478197735	
2	7541	
3	2871	
4	2991	
5	820324	
6	2134	
7	817102	
8	44272233	
9	46344341	
10	461435	
11	43802340	
12	579773	
13	817283	
14	872840	
15	432209	
16	46333422	
17	323823	
18	371153	
19		

Number of medical cards herein ___

Number of personal papers herein ___

Book Mark _____

See also _____

| 4 | **3 Mid. Infantry.** (Lillard's.) | **Tenn.** |

James R. Walker

Sergt., Co. C, 3 Reg't Tennessee Vols.

Appears on

Company Muster Roll

of the organization named above,

for *Sept. & Oct.* , 186 .

Enlisted:

When , 186 .

Where

By whom

Period

Last paid:

By whom

To what time 186 .

Present or absent *Present*

Remarks:

Name appears on column of

persons present James B. Walker

Book mark:

G. E. Hernandez

(542) Copyist.

(Confederate.)

3 Mid. Infantry. (Liberd's) | **Tenn.**

James L. Walker

Serg't, Co. ___, 3 Reg't Tennessee Vols.

Appears on

Company Muster Roll

of the organization named above,

for _Nov & Dec_ , 186_ .

Enlisted:

When _May 8_ , 186_ .

Where _Calhoun Tenn_

By whom _H. Bill_

Period _12 mos_

Last paid:

By whom _C W M McElrath_

To what time _Oct 31_ , 186_ .

Present or absent _Present_

Remarks: _____

_____

_____

_____

The M (Liberd's) Regiment Tennessee Mounted Infantry was
organized May 26, 1863, and was mustered into the service of the
Confederate States June 6, 1863. It was re-organized May 14,
1864, when (1st) Company K was transferred to the 6th Regiment
Tennessee Infantry and became Company E of that organization.
(2d) Company K was then formed of men who had been transferred from Company H of this regiment. The organization was
mounted about January 1, 1864.

Book mark: _____

C. C. Fernandez

(642) Copyist.

| H | 3 Mid. Infantry.
(Lillard's.) | Tenn. |

James V. Walker

_____, Co. _____, 3 Reg't Tennessee Vols.

Appears on

Company Muster Roll

of the organization named above,

for _June & Feb_ , 186_.

Enlisted:

When _May 8_ , 186_.

Where _Exchange, Ten_

By whom _H. Hill_

Period _12 mos_

Last paid:

By whom _C. M. O. McElrath_

To what time _June 1_ , 186_

Present or absent _Present_

Remarks: _____

_____

_____

_____

The 3d (Lillard's) Regiment Tennessee Mounted Infantry was
organized May 20, 1861, and was mustered into the service of the
Confederate States June 9, 1861. It was re-organized May 14,
1862, when (1st) Company K was transferred to the Old Regiment
Tennessee Infantry and became Company E of that organization.
(2d) Company K was then formed of men who had been transferred from Company B of this regiment. The organization was
mounted about January 1, 1864.

Book mark: _____

G. E. Hennessy

(642)   Copyist.

| *H* | 3 Mtd. Infantry. | **Tenn.** |
| | (Lillard's.) | |

J. V. Walker

Lieut , Co. *G* , 3 Reg't Tennessee Vols.

Appears on

Company Muster Roll

of the organization named above,

for *May 1 to Aug. 31* , 186 *3* .

Enlisted:

When _____ , 186 .

Where _____

By whom _____

Period _____

Last paid:

By whom _____

To what time _____ , 186 .

Present or absent *Not stated*

Remarks: _____

_____

_____

Supra Roll is ready the Co.

The 3d (Lillard's) Regiment Tennessee Mounted Infantry was organized May 20, 1861, and was mustered into the service of the Confederate States June 6, 1861. It was re-organized May 14, 1862, when (1st) Company K was transferred to the 6th Regiment Tennessee Infantry and became Company E of that organization. (2d) Company K was then formed of men who had been transferred from Company H of this regiment. The organization was mounted about January 1, 1864.

Book mark: _____

G. E. Fernandez

(642)   Copyist.

N | 3 Md. Infantry. (Lillard's.) | Tenn.

J. C. Walker

Lieut., Co. *B*, 3 Reg't Tennessee Vols.

Appears on

Company Muster Roll

of the organization named above,

for *Sept. 1 to Dec. 31*, 186_7_?

Enlisted:

When _____, 186_.

Where _____

By whom _____

Period _____

Last paid:

By whom _____

To what time _____, 186_.

Present or absent *Absent*

Remarks: *Absent on Detached Service getting up absentees*

The 3d (Lillard's) Regiment Tennessee Mounted Infantry was organized May 26, 1861, and was mustered into the service of the Confederate States June 8, 1861. It was re-organized May 14, 1862, when (1st) Company K was transferred to the Old Regiment Tennessee Infantry and became Company E of that organization. (2d) Company K was then formed of men who had been transferred from Company H of this regiment. The organization was mounted about January 1, 1864.

Book mark: _____

(642)

G. C. Howards, Copyist.

3 Mtd. Infantry.
(Lillard's.)

Tenn.

J. E. Walker

1 Lieut, Co. G, 3 Regiment Tennessee Cavalry.

Appears on

Company Muster Roll

of the organization named above,

for *June 1 to June 30,* 1864.

Enlisted:

When _____ , 186 .

Where _____

By whom _____

Period _____

Last paid:

By whom _____

To what time _____ , 186 .

Present or absent *Absent*

Remarks: *A prisoner of war*

_____

_____

_____

The 3d (Lillard's) Regiment Tennessee Mounted Infantry was organized May 30, 1861, and was mustered into the service of the Confederate States June 6, 1861. It was re-organized May 14, 1862, when (1st) Company K was transferred to the 5th Regiment Tennessee Infantry and became Company E of that organization. (2d) Company K was then formed of men who had been transferred from Company H of this regiment. The organization was mounted about January 1, 1864.

Book mark:

G. E. Hernandez

(642) Copyist.

3 Mid. Infantry. | **Tenn.**
(Lillard's.)

J. V. Walker

(1st Lieut., Co. G , 3 Regiment Tennessee Cavalry.

Appears on a

Roster

of the 3rd Regiment of Tennessee Cavalry Volunteers, Vaughn's Brigade, Army of S. W. Va. and E. Tenn. Organized May 29, 1861. Mustered into Confederate service June 6, 1861, for 12 months.

Roster dated *Hd Qrs Forces E Tenn*

Oct 24 , 186*1*.

Date of entry or muster } into State service, } , 186 .

Date of entry or muster } into Confederate service, } , 186 .

Date of rank, and whether } by appointment, election } *Elected* or promotion, } *May 14* 186*2*.

Date and cause } of vacancy, } , 186 .

Name of successor

Remarks: *In Northern Prison*

The 3d (Lillard's) Regiment Tennessee Mounted Infantry was organized May 29, 1861, and was mustered into the service of the Confederate States June 6, 1861. It was re-organized May 14, 1862, when (1st) Company K was transferred to the 59th Regiment Tennessee Infantry and became Company E of that organization. (3d) Company K was then formed of men who had been transferred from Company H of this regiment. The organization was mounted about January 1, 1864.

Book mark :

J. Funk

(948) Copyist.

Ur   3   Tenn.

J. T. Walker

Private, Co. *G* , 3 Reg't Tennessee Infantry

Appears on a

Roll of Prisoners of War

paroled at Vicksburg, Miss., according to the terms of capitulation entered into by the commanding Generals of the United States and Confederate forces July 4, 1863.

Roll dated _____ *not dated*

Paroled at Vicksburg, Miss., July 10, 1863.

Where captured *Vicksburg, Miss.*

When captured *July 4*, 186 *3*.

Remarks: _____

_____

_____

_____

_____

_____

_____

_____

_____

_____

_____

_____

74

M. Blade

(659b)   Copyist.

H 3 Tenn

James W. Walker
1 Lieut. Co. G 3 Regt. Tenn. Inf.

Appears on a register of

Prisoners of War,

Department of the Cumberland.

When captured _Feby 1_ , 1864

Where captured _Murray Co. Ga_

By whom captured

When paroled _____ , 186_

To what point forwarded _Louisville Ky_
Feby 11 1864.

Remarks: _For exchange._

Dept. of the Cumberland, Reg. No. 2; page 249
(Hd. Qrs. Prov. Mar. General, Nashville, Tenn.)

J. Boyd

(639.)   Copyist.

N

James V. Walter
1 Lieut. C. S. 3 Regt. Tenn. Inf.

Appears on a

Roll of Prisoners of War

at Nashville, Tenn., captured by forces under
Maj. Gen. Thomas, commanding Dept. of the
Cumberland, and forwarded to Capt. Stephen
E. Jones, Pro. Mar. Gen., Louisville, Ky.,
February 11, 1864.

Roll dated Headquarters Dept. Cumberland,
Office Provost Marshal General, Nashville,
Tenn., February 11, 1864.

Where captured *Murry Co., Ga.*

When captured *Feb. 1*, 186*4*

Remarks:

Hd. Qrs. Prov. Mar. Gen'l, Dept. of the Cumb'd,
Nashville, Tenn.; Roll No. **203.**

J. A. McLaughlin

(629b)   Copyist.

(Confederate.)

Pvt. | 3 | Tenn.

John W. Walker

Pvt. Co. F. 3 Regt. Tenn. Inf.

Appears on a

Roll of Prisoners of War

received at Louisville, Ky., Military Prison during five days ending Feb. 15, 1864 *

Roll dated Office Pro. Mar. Genl., Dist. of Ky., Louisville, Feb. 16, 1864.

Where captured Marion Co. Tenn.

When captured Feb. 1, 1864.

Where sent Camp Chase Ohio

When Feb. 16, 1864.

Remarks:

* Duplicate roll (which is incomplete) shows that the men whose names are borne on this roll were received from Nashville, Tenn.

Number of roll:

119; sheet 1

(639b) Copyist.

(Confederate.)

[illegible] | 2 | [illegible]

[illegible]

[illegible]

Appears on a Register of

Prisoners of War

received at Military Prison, Louisville, Ky.

Where captured [illegible]

When captured [illegible], 186[illegible].

Discharged:

Terms [illegible]

When [illegible], 186[illegible].

Remarks:

Louisville, Ky., Register No. 2; page [illegible]

[illegible]

(639) *Copyist.*

N | 3 | Tenn

James V. Hulter

1 Lieut Co. G 3 Regt. Tenn Infy

Appears on a roll of

Prisoners of War

at Military Prison, Louisville, Ky.

Date when received *Feb. 11*, 1864.

Where captured *Murray Co. Ga.*

Date when captured *Feb. 1*, 1864.

Date when discharged *Feb. 13*, 1864.

Where sent *Camp Chase, O.*

Remarks, charges, &c.:

from Nashville.

Louisville, Ky., Register No. 6; page *25*.

E. C. Rankin

(689)   Copyist.

W   3   Tenn.

James V. Walker,

1ˢᵗ Lt. Co. G, 3 Reg. Tenn. Inf.

Appears on a

Roll of Prisoners of War

forwarded from Louisville Military Prison
Camp Chase, Ohio, Feb. 13, 1864.

Roll dated Office Pro. Mar. Gen'l, District of
Kentucky, Louisville, Feb. 13, 1864.

Where captured *Munroy Co., Ga.*

When captured *Feby. 1*, 1864.

Remarks:

Number of roll:

400

J. T. Hinsley

(6393)   Copyist.

N~ J. Tenn

James V. Walker
1 Lt., Co. C, 3 Regt Tenn Cav

Appears on a Descriptive Roll of

Prisoners of War

at Camp Chase, Ohio,

Arrested:
Where _____ Murray co Ga

When _____ Feb 1 , 1864.

Received at Camp Chase, Ohio,
When _____ Feb 13 , 1864.

Whence _____ Louisville Ky

By whose order _____ Brig Gen Carson

Description:

Height _____ ft. _____ in.; age _____

Eyes _____ ; hair _____ ; complexion _____

Date of departure _____ Mch 23 1864.

Remarks: Transferred to Ft.
Delaware

_____

_____

_____

_____

Camp Chase, Ohio, Register No. 2; page 452.

A Moseley

Copyist.

N | 3 | Tenn

Jno V Walker
1 Lieut A G 3 Regt Ten Inf

Appears on a

Roll of Prisoners of War

received at Fort Delaware, Del., from Camp
Chase, Ohio, and Ohio Penitentiary, March 2?,
1864.

Roll dated _Not dated_

_____, 186_

Where captured _Murray Co Ga_

When captured _Feby 1_ , 1864

Remarks: _____

Number of roll:
31 5 sheet _____

(629b)   Copyist.

W   3   Penn.

J. V. Walker

1 Lt. Co. J, 3 Reg't Tenne Inf.

Appears on a register of

Prisoners of War

at Fort Delaware, Del.

Where captured _Murray Co. Geo_

When captured _Feby 1_ , 186 4

When joined post _March 27_ , 186 4

Remarks:

Fort Delaware, Del., Register No. 4; page 57

(439)   J V B Dowd   Copyist.

W | 3 | Tenn.

J. W. Walker,

1st Lieut. 3 Regt. Tenn.

Name appears as signature to an

Oath of Allegiance

to the United States, subscribed to at Fort
Delaware, Del.

Place of residence McMinn, Tenn.

Complexion Dark ; hair Dark.

Eyes Grey ; height 5 ft. 7 in.

REMARK: "Released June 16, '65, In accord-
ance with Genl. Orders 109, War Dep., A. G. O.,
June 6, '65."*

Remarks: ....

....

....

....

....

....

....

....

....

....

....

....

....

*Taken from incomplete duplicate roll.

Number of roll:

189; sheet 12

J. Hundly

(600)

| W | 3 | Tenn. |

J. W. Walker
1 Lt. Co. G. 3. Regt. Tenn.

Appears on a

Register

containing Rosters of Commissioned Officers, Provisional Army Confederate States.

Date of appointment May 14. , 1862

Date of resignation, death, transfer or promotion }

, 186

Remarks :

Confed. Arch., Chap. 1, File No. 92, page 130

J. Cary

Copyist

| 2/. | 3 | Tenn |

J. V. Walker

1" Lieut, 3 Reg't Tenn. Vol.

Appears on an

Abstract of Payments

made by Geo. W. Allen, Capt. and A. Q. M., 3d
Tenn. Volunteers, for the months of May, 1863,
to February, 1864.

Abstract dated Hickory Station, N.C.,
Apr 27 , 186 4

Date of payment Sept. 30 , 1863.

From Aug 1 , 1863.

To Aug 31 , 1863.

Amount $ 90, 00

Remarks:

Book mark:

J. P. Brown

(468) Copyist.

W | 3 | Tenn

J. W. Walker

A. Lieut. 3 Regt Tenn. Vol.

Appears on an

Abstract of Payments

made by Geo. W. Allen, Capt. and A. Q. M., 3d
Tenn. Volunteers, for the months of May, 1863,
to February, 1864.

Abstract dated _Hickory Station, Ga,_

Apr 27, 1864.

Date of payment _Jany 15_, 1864.

From _Sept 1_, 1863.

To _Dec 31_, 1863.

Amount $ _360, 00_

Remarks:

Book mark:

(68*)   _J. Brown_   Copyist.

Voucher No.

Pay the .... day of .... 186..

....

.... U. S.

From the .... day of .... 186..

To the .... day of .... 186..

Pay .... $ ....

Forage ....

———————————

Amount .... $ ....

Voucher No 26 Abstr B, 2 Qr 1862

SPECIAL REQUISITION.

* * *

Co. D. 8th Tennessee

.

Quartermaster

May 29th 1862

VOUCHER NO.

Paid the ___ day of _January_ 1865

1st Lt. _James S. H. Brackett_

_goes Regt. Tyga ___ C. S._

From the ___ day of ___ 1864

To the _31st_ day of _Dec_ 1865

∴

Pay ___ _5.00_ $

Forage ___

Amount $ _5.00_ $

REQUISITION

FOR

Clothing and Camp Equipage.

A. J. Tinker for A.

Commanding Company.

Sept 30th 186

3 Tenn

Requisition for Clothing and Camp Equipage.

For Company _G_ 7th Reg't. Ela. Vols., Commanded by _Col. _____

Articles.	No.	Remarks.	Prices.
Hats or Caps,			
Coats or Jackets,			
Overcoats,			
Pants, Pairs of			
Shirts,			
Socks, Pairs of			
Blankets,			
Shoes, Pairs of			
Drawers, Pairs of			
Tents, Common or Wall,	1		
Axes,	1		
Camp Kettles,	2		
Spades or Shovels,			
Sabers and Lids,	1		
Skillets and Lids,			

I Certify that the above Requisition is correct, and that the articles specified are absolutely necessary for my Company.

_____ Commanding

_____, Quartermaster, will issue the articles above specified.

_____ Commanding Post.

Received at _____, the ____ day of _____, 1863,

of _____, Quartermaster, the Clothing, &c., in full of the above requisition.

[SIGNED DUPLICATE.]

105

Walker J. V.

Lieut, Co. L, 3d (Vol) Tenn.,
Regt

(Confederate.)

Inclosures.

Bed Cards	Final Statements
Burial Records	Furloughs or L. of A.
Certs. of Dis. for Discharge	Med. Certificates
C. M. Charges	Med. Des. Lists
Descriptive Lists	Orders
Discharge Certificates	Pris. of War Record
Enlistment Papers	Resignations

Other papers relating to—

Admission to Hosp'l	Furlough or L. of A.
Casualty Sheet	Med. Examination
Confinement	Misc. Information
Contracts	Pay or Clothing
Death or Effects	Personal Reports
Desertion	Rank
Discharge from Hosp'l	Transfer to Hosp'l
Discharge from Service	Transportation
Duty	

Appendix E

Fort Delaware Military Prison

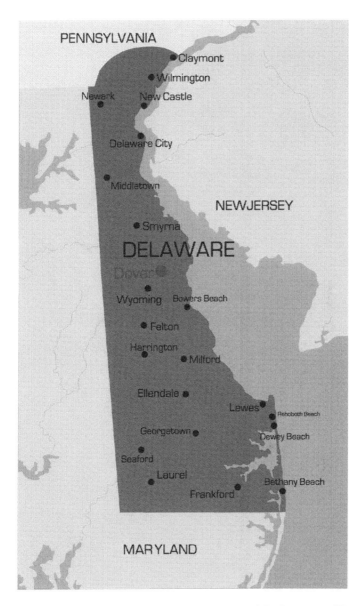

Fort Delaware was located just east of Delaware City

Fort Delaware

[Source: Library of Congress HAER DEL,2-DELAC.V,1—1]

East Side with Bridge and Bastion

[SOURCE: Library of Congress HABS DEL,2-PEPIS,1—1]

West Side, Gorge Facade with Casemate and Barbette Fenestration
[Source: Library of Congress HABS DEL,2-PEPIS,1—2]

West Side with Sally Port

[Source: **Library of Congress** HABS DEL,2-PEPIS,1—8]

Sally Port Entrance Exterior Detail
[Source: Library of Congress HABS DEL,2-PEPIS,1—7]

Entrance to Sally Port, Interior

[Source: Library of Congress HABS DEL,2-PEPIS,1—22]

Parade Ground with Officers' Quarters, Looking West

[Source: Library of Congress HABS DEL,2-PEPIS,1—12]

Squad Room

[Source: Library of Congress HABS DEL,2-PEPIS,1—37]

Officers' Quarters, Interior

[Source: Library of Congress HABS DEL,2-PEPIS,1—36]

Northeast Stairtower and Casemates
[Source: Library of Congress HABS DEL,2-PEPIS,1—15]

Appendix F

The Original Diary of
Lieutenant James Vance Walker

U.S. Millitary Prison. Officers Barracks
Fort. Delaware. Delaware.

We design in the preceding sketches to show as familiar as possible the rise and progress of the religious element in our midst during the first three months of our confinement on this Island. And the gradual developement of those christian graces that ought always to caracterize the disciples of our Lord and Master. We feel a deep sense of our inability to do justice to a subject so very important. So let these few preliminary remarks suffice. And we will begin back at the time of our departure from Camp, Chase Ohio,

On Friday March 25th 1864 two hundred and seventy two Confederate Officers held as prisoners of was at Camp Chase Ohio. left that post heavily guarded by the 88th Ohio Inft Regt They were marched to the depot at Columbus, where transportation awaited them to this Island. at the railroad station they were joined by the sixty nine Officers from Brig Genl John H. Morgans Cavalry Command. who had suffered a long and painful incarceration in the Ohio State prison. Soon they were on their journey hither. buoyant with the hope that they were homeward bound, and would soon reach the soil of their own beloved country. So manfully struggling to drive an unrelenting foe from her borders. We were so closely guarded that we could only catch an occasional glimpse of the yankee land as we passed along. About 2 Oclock P.M. on sunday March 27th we arrived at Philadelphia where an immense multitude of the curious had assembled to see those who had endured so much for their bleeding country. We were marched on board the Steamer Oscola; and as our vessel moved off into the Delaware river deafning cheers were raised for the land of Dixie while the gazeing multitude were left on the shore. We arrived at this post about 8 Oclock P.m. and occupied quarters previously prepared for us. The first few weeks at Fort Delaware is indeed a sad picture to be drawn, the occurences of that time are not such as should appear on these pages except so far as may be necessary to show the moral condition of our fellowprisoners at that time. Intoxicating liquors were sold by the Suttler, and their use was so excessive that it threatened the overthrow of every moral and social ventue amongst us. In former days we had witneped the withering and blighting influences of this monster evil on society. We have seen him enter the quiet and happy home circle. and with one stroke of his arm of iron dash in pieces the family altar and take up his abode where peace and love had howered so long. We have seen society wither under his scorching breath, and the hopes of many a fond mother crushed and end in despair. We have seen all the tender sensibilities of man's nature distroyed and his heart steeped in the verey fumes hell by this agent for evil. And here again, while strangers in a strange land and in Prison we behold his desolating effects. The only apparent bond of union amongst us was our devotion to the cause of our common country, and this was too week to stand the test of the monster, in many instances, and personal difficulties were of frequent occurence. This traffic was carried on solely for the sake of gain; and daily we witnessed the sad specticle of seeing the souls of our fellow men placed in human balances and weighed against gold and silver. Would that we could stop here; but other kindred vices no less degrading in the eyes of an allwise God were practiced unceasingly. Gambling in all its forms were practiced without mitigation. The gambling tables were set in every Divivision room, Surrounded by the unfortunate vicims to this habit from morning until a late hour at night. Cursing was the common dialect of the camp. At almost every breath we could hear the name of the Lord God taken in vain. The number of proffessing christians, afterwards found to be forty, were scarcely known or recognized as such. They yeilded in a grater or less degree to the influences around them. They not unfrequently could be seen around the gaming tables interested in the varying fortunes of the gambler. Some went so far as to pertieipate in the games. It is however important to state that there was a few who stood aloof from these vices; and whose hearts were daily lifted to God for a revival of christian piety in our midst. The man of God thus beholding the desolations of our Zion could but exclaim in the anguish of his Soul, "There is none that seeketh after God," They are all gone out of the way, they are together become unprofitable, there is none that doeth good no not one. This brief allusion to the universal prevalence of wickedness among the impenitent and lukewarmness among the believers; will suffice to show our extreme moral desolation. Among the forty christians before mentioned there was one minister Capt A.M. Samford of the 14th Texas Cavalry. He had labored for the good of Souls at Camp Chase; but failed to arouse believers from the deadly sin of apathy which had seized their hearts. But he was not dispondant, Like a faithful sentinal on the watch towers of Zion he continued to Labor. On sunday morning April 3rd divine service was held for the first time, in division 29. The audience was silent and attentive, while Capt Samford preached from the following text. Thou shall love the Lord thy God with all thy heart and with all thy soul and with all thy strength and with all thy mind and thy neighbor as thy self." He showed the necessity of devoting our lives to the service of God and presenting our bodies as a living sacrifice through our Lord and Savior Jesus Christ. In the evening Capt Stamford preached again in Division 27, from Zech. 4. 6. At the conclusion of his second discourse an event occured which subsequently led to great results. The Rev Dr Isaac W. K. Handy of Portsmouth Va. was permitted to visit our barracks from the Fort, where he had suffered a painful imprisonment for more than nine months for conscience sake". At the request of many he preached, from Jere. 18th 9th "The heart is deceitful above all things and desperately wicked. Thus ere our first Sabbath at Fort Delaware had passt away, a third sermon had been delivered. Notwithstanding the Giver of all good had so bountifully blest us with the means of grace, it is sad to state that while these services were being conducted, the card table was set and well attended in other Divisions, in violation of the plain language of the Decalogue. Remember the sabbath day to keep it holy." During the insuing week these three sermons were productive of no results that were perceptable. Our condition remained as previously depicted, but steps were taken to arouse believers from their lethargy. At the suggestion of Dr Handy a roll of the church members was made, when it was found that only forty had reported their names. On Saturday the 9th of April a number of Testaments Episcopal Prayerbooks tract and religious papers were sent into the barracks for distribution, Dr Handy was permitted to visit us again on Sunday the 10th April and preached a very interesting and instructive sermon from 1st Cor. 9th 24th "So run that you may obtain!" At this meeting he announced his purpose to preach for us every Sunday if agreeable, and also that he had effected arrangements to visit us during the week at which time he would be happy to converse with any who felt an interest in their souls salvation, if they would but let him know who they were. He urged christians to go to work, and labor for the good of souls. Pointing to our field of labor he would with the deepest interest speak of the good that might be accomplished if we would only labor as it becometh good soldiers of the cross. The manifestation of this interest in our welfare began to beget an interest in the hearts of the christians, and a few were aroused to a more active discharge of their duties, but the influence on the unconverted was so far imperceptible, as will be shown hereafter. The first evidence of an increased interest in religion was the organization of a nightly prayermeeting. This prayermeeting was organized at the suggestion of Capt W.C. Shane who had found Jesus precious to his soul while in close confinement at the Ohio Penitentiary. There alone in his cell, the truth of God penetrated his soul and he was brought to a knowledge of the truth as it is in Christ Jesus." His conference Capt Samford on this subject resulted in the determination of holding a prayer meeting nightly which at first, was conducted privately, but few of the brethren having any knowledge of its existance. The first meeting was held on the night of April the 11th and was participated in by Maj. Bullock. Capt. Tracy. Capt. Bennett, Capt. Moon, Capt. Moses. in addition to the two brethren already mentioned. The division in which these meeting were held was destitute of stove and benches, and the weather was disagreeably cold. But those faithful brethren were not to be deterred from their labors but continued to meet each other promptly at the place appointed, however inclement the night, their devotions to Almighty God assended to heaven. The earnest petitions of these disciples of our Lord were unitedly borne to a throne of grace for a revival of religion in our prison. And most graciously did He bless their efforts. These meeting were soon generally known and were quite largely attended, and in proportion to the increase of attendants the deeper and more extended was the interest manifested. during the first week in May the meetings were so largely attended and the interest so increased, that it was thought advisable to extend the privileges and blessing more fully to the unconverted. Accordingly on May the 9th an invitation was extended to all who felt an interest in their souls eternal welfare and desired God's people to pray for them to come forward and let the fact be known. Four mourners came forward in response to this call. Thus the hearts of christians were made to rejoice. On the day following the same invitation was extended but ere Capt Samford could end his earnest appeal for all to come and live, the meetings dispersed by the Federal authorities and all present informed that meetings for religious worship would be prohibited in future untill further orders. Thus at a time when our meetings were being especially blest by the outpouring of God's love and mercy, by an intervention of human authority they were discontinued. Up to this time Dr Handy had been visiting us regularly during the week.

conducting our prayer meetings and conversing with all on the subject of
religion who winced an interest on the subject. In the mean time the
religious element was largely on the increase. The sale of spirituous liquors
had in a measure been stoped. Gambling to a considerable extent had abated.
Swearing was still common but to a considerable extent checked by the religious
influences brought to beare. It will not be improper to state in this connection that sometime prior to this, a library of several hundred volumes
known as the Prisoners library at Fort Delaware; had been sent us
by ladies of Philadelphia which proved a valuable auxiliery to tho-
-se who were laboring so earnestly for a reformation in our barracks.
Those who had been seen at the card table on the Lord day being now
supplied with reading matter devoted sundays to reading and
attending devine service. Many backsliders who had wandered far
from the path of duty, and had become so blinded by the "god of this world"
that they had forgotten they were purged from their old sins" were
brought back to the fold of Christ and began labor afresh in His vineyard.
The influence on the unconverted was much greater than was at first
supposed. some who had not presented themselves publicly as subjects
of prayer had mad their requests known to their friends privately.
Others communicated their convictions of sin in writing and asked an
interest in the prayers of the church. these communications being alwa-
-ys read at the prayer meetings. Such was the state of religious feel-
-ing in our midst when we were prohibited from assembling ourselves
together to worship the Giver of every good and perfect gift.

We now ask you to go back with us two days. prior to the suppression
of the public worship of God by the federals, while we dwell for a
moment on The first Communion of the disciples of Christ at
Fort Delaware. On Sunday morning May 8th as usual Dr Handy
was admitted to our barracks, and preached from the following Text.
"Ye cannot drink the cup of the Lord and the cup of devils; ye cannot
be pertakers of the Lord's table and of the table of devils." 1st Cor 10th 21.
Our venerable brother dwelt at length on christian consistency,
urging with great earnestness and zeal that the followers of Christ
should avoid even the very appearance of evil. That they should
deny themselves all worldly lusts, and cleave to that which was good
as it becometh the peculiar people of God. At the conclusion of

125

the sermon all christians of what ever denomination were invited to meet with the brethren in the evening and commemorate the sufferings and death of our Saviour at the communion table. An invitation was also given to any who had experienced a change of heart and had not connected themselves with any church to come forward and be received into the church at large if they desired it. Also any who desired to receive the ordinance of baptism to make their request known and it could be attended to at once. At the time appointed in the evening a large and attentive audience had assembled to witness the disciples partake of the emblems of the broken body and shed blood of our Lord and Saviour Jesus Christ.

The following brethren made application for admission into the church and were unanimously received into full fellowship. Capt. W. R. White. of Ark. Lieut. p. F. Caldwell of Mo. Lieut. T. p. Hardee. of Ga. Sgt. C. V. Cyrus. of Tenn. The two latter brethren were at their request baptized according to the custom of the Presbyterian church. After a short discourse from Dr. Handy explanitory of the institution they were about to observe, urging each one to examin himself and so let him eat." the elements were produced and administered to the brethren in a sitting posture. The patriarchal appearance of Dr. Handy, his deeply fervent tones as he repeated the words of his Master, "Take eat this is my body; and the tearful eyes and the bowed heads of the communicants as the loaf and cup was passed amongst them, made this a most solemn and interesting scene. It cannot soon be forgotten by those witnessed it. This meeting was not only a solemn and interesting one. but it proved beneficial as a means of "groth in grace" The announcement that an opportunity would be afforded for all christians to meet in holy communion around the sacramental board was made more than a week prior to its observance.

This announcement crowded the christian's memory with the joys and blessings bestowed on him by his Heavenly Father in former days while showing fort the Lords death till he comes in the observence of this holy institution; and he paused and looked within himself and searched his heart as with a lighted candle. Dr Handy visited the barracks twice during the preceeding

week and conversed with many on the subject of this communion.
urging them to make a most rigid self examination and to
engage continually in prayer to God. By this means the brethren
were fully aroused and saw themselves in their proper light,
and as they moved among their comrades they began to scatter
broad cast the seeds of life, and while some fell by the way side
and in stoney places, others fell in good ground and brought
fort fruit to the honor and glory of God. We now resume our nara-
tive where we left off, the prohibition of public worship by the
Federal authorities. The regular prayermeetings were again
commenced on saturday may the 14th Capt Shane and others having obtained permission to continue public worship in a
diffrent Division. On sunday May 15th there was no preaching
in the barracks. Dr Handy being prohibited from visiting us as
usual and Capt Samford thinking it best owing to the recent
interference by the authorities to omit Services on that day.
On the evening of the same day howeve. Dr Handy and the political prisoners confined in the Cort were sent into our barracks
and assigned quarters. The great laborer was thus ushered into the harvest field. He was now transferred to the midst of
those for whose spiritual welfare he was so much concerned
and for whom he labored so devotedly. If the three days interruption of religious services, checked the good work which had
commenced, the accession of Dr Handy to those engaged in it,
more than compensated for the lost ground. Indeed the daily
intercourse of this venerable brother among us was productive of great
Spiritual good. He believed wherever God sent him; there he intended for him to labor. So he entered with all his mind and strength
into the work before him. Prayermeeting was held on this same evening conducted by him; and at which the first conversion was announced. On may the 19th one hundred and sixty Officers captured during
the battle in the wilderness arrived and confined in our barracks.
among them were many brethren and one minister Capt T. W. Harris
of the 12th Ga. The church members immediately enrolled their names

127

and active participated in our religious exercises. Capt Harris also began to labor in the capacity of a minister. On Friday May the 20th an enquiry meeting was organized at the suggestion of Dr Handy. These meetings were held every morning at 10 O'Clock and proved a great blessing especially to backsliders who were anxious to renew their vows to their Lord. Here they were met by the ministers and brethren, and freely conversed with each other in regard to their true moral condition. The exercises at these meetings usually consisted of singing, prayer, reading the scriptures and religious conversation. Many who had been long luke warm in the service of his master will thank God in all time to come that they attended the Enquiry meeting at Fort Delaware. On this also was organized a noonday prayer meeting. The primary object of this meeting was to invoke God's blessings upon the church for strengthning christians for their growth in grace and an increase in faith; that they might be the better instruments in the hands of God for doing good. But four persons were present at its organization. Capt Shane at whose suggestion it was instituted being one of the number. But at each succeeding meeting the number gradually increased until all the active members of the church were regular attendants. The exercises of these meetings were the same as those of the meetings of Enquiry. Singing, prayer reading scriptures and religious experience. On June the 25th the time of meeting was changed to morning instead of noon. On May the 26 in the evening another prayer meeting was organized Capt G.W. Moor W R White and W C Shane. These brethren designed their meetings to be private. They remained in the chapel after the dismisal of regular prayer meeting to pray with and for each other. For several evenings they kept their meeting strictly secret, but soon others were admitted. until their meetings numbered 10 or 12 brethren. These meeting were kept up as long as a place of meeting could be obtained. Two or three mourners would remain each night with these brethren to be prayed for. They often remained in secrete communion with their God until the night was far spent. and it was not unfrequently the case that mourners heavily laden with sin came fort from these meetings new creatures in Christ Jesus. It was not long after this meeting was established until another prayermeeting was organized: at the suggestion of Dr. Handy. it was instituted exclusively for young Converts whome there were at this time about twenty. These meeting were conducted by the young brethren alternately; none others attending. The exercises being the same as those of the Enquiry meeting. The revival was now in full progress. Dr Handy's daily labors commencing on the 13th Capt Harris arrived on the 19th accompanied by a large number of energetic Christians: and all uniting their efforts to advance the kingdom of Christ, the good cause received additional strength and gradually increased until great good was accomplished.

One interesting feature of this revival was the absence of excitement common on such occasions. convictions were silent and deep: and conversions calm and thorough. Christians at all times were fervent in the spirit serving the Lord. Brethren of all denominations assisted in the exercises. No party lines were drawn or known but all labored together cheerfully in the Lord's vineyard: and God vouchsafed his spirit in answer to the petitions of his servents and its blest influence was felt by both saint and sinner. Thursday June 9th was set apart as a day of Fasting Humiliation and prayer for the outpouring of Gods holy spirit on the whole island and to invoke the mercies and blessings of God upon our bleeding Country the Confederate States of America. This day was observed as such by all christians, and during the day prayers were continually ascending from more than a hundred hearts to a throne of grace for their sinful comrades and desolated Country. These prayers were abundantly answered in the conversion of Sinners and the building up of Christians. June 25th was a day appointed for the examination of applicants for admission into the church at large by Dr. Handy Capt Lamford and Capt Harris. But the day prior to this we were notified by the authorities that Six hundred prisoners of war from Pt Lookout Md be here and the room then used for a chapel must be given up. This was the only interruption of our meetings since the 10th of May and plans were soon put on foot to remedy this. The number of conversions up to this time was about thirty and others still enquiring the

way to Jesus; And to prevent a complete cessation of religious
exercises. Seventy brethren agreed to occupy a Division and
permit the regular daily exercises to be conducted in their
Division. and thus religious worship was kept up as before
after a slight interruption. In the meantime. the examin-
-ation of the young. converts was not lost sight of. But at the
time appointed. a committee composed of Dr Handy. Capt. Sam-
-ford Capt Harris. Capt Tracy and Capt Eastin, and Maj Bullock.
these brethren representing the different Churches. assembled
and examined the applicants. This examination was not
conducted according the established form of any particular
church; but each member of the committee was expected to ask
such questions as he thought necessary until all were satisf-
-ied when. the vote was taken for the admission or rejection of
the brethren. There was thirty brethren examined and all
decided by the committee to be fit subjects for church memb-
-ership. and were so reported by the committee the day follow-
-ing. As was anticipated Six hundred Officers Prisoners of War
arrived here from Pt Lookout to day the 25th June. of this
large accession of prisoners there was two ministers Lieut
D. P. Thomas of Ten— and Lt G W Carter of ark. and a large
number of professors of Christianity. Some of them had
been Confined. before their removal to Pt Lookout. at Johnson's Island
and had there proticipated in a glorious revival of religion. and
while at Pt Lookout their labors had been kept up to some
extent They entered heartily in to the work with us and
labored for the good of souls. X [The second communion's] Sunday June 26th will be
long remembered by many of us, Dr Handy an elegant
sermon from the text our profession" in the morning.
The discourse was an earnest admonition for all believers to at-
-tach themselves to some one of the evangelical Churches, and take a
decided stand on the Lord's Side. Showing the Church to be the pro-
-per place. and safest place for believers. At the conclusion of the
Morning Services it was announced that the Lord's supper
would be administered in the evening at 3 O'Clock. Accordingly
at the time appointed a large majority of the prisoners in the barracks

assembled in the open air to witness or participate in the celebration
of the Lord's Sufferings and death. Dr Handy who might be called
verey appropriately the Chaplain for the Confederate Officers at
Fort Delaware. Conducted the meeting. After the usual preliminary
exercises and a few brief remarks explanatory nature design and im-
-portance of the holy institution about to be observed. he proceeded
to receive publically into the Church at large the converts who had
been examined by the Committee on the day before. These as their
names were called cameforward and arranged themselves around
the alter where the usual questions were propounded and answered.
After which they were by a unanimous vote received into full fell
-owship. The following is a list of names rank and residence of
those thus received. W. F. Aud. Political Prisoner, Poolesville Md.
A H Baily Lieut 14th Va. cav. T. W. Bullitt. Lieut 2nd Ky cav.
Baker Lieut 3rd Ky cavl. Plattsburg Md. E. L. Bell, Lieut 10th Va Surrey Va
J. F. Caldwell Lieut 8th Mo cavl. Dallas Mo. P. B. Davis Lieut 14 Ga Jackson
A. H. Edgar, Capt 29th Va Lewisburg Va. J H Guthrie Lieut 10th Va
Pinkneyville Ala. W. F. Gorden, Capt Jenkins cavl. Clarksburg va
F. Holmes Lieut 29 Miss. Hornelake Miss. Jasper Horne Lieut 9th Ten
Columbia Tenn. W. L. Hunter Lieut 43rd Va Wayensboro Va. H L W.
Johnson Capt 12th ark. Okolona. ark. G. W. Kurty Capt 5th Va Winchester
J. F. Lytton, Capt 5th Va Long Glade Va P. L. Mays, Lieut 19th Ark.
Fayetteville ark. W. H. Morris. Lieut 2nd Ky cavl. Lexington Ky P. T. Mackey.
Lieut 48th Ten Columbia Tenn F. H. McChristion Lieut. Huntsville ark.
H. M. Middleton Capt 38th Ga. Somerville Ga F. Noble Lieut 3rd Texas
Alvoa, Texas, John Paul Lieut 1st Va cavl. W. F. Robbins Capt 28 ala.
H Reed Maj Miss cavl. B. Roberts Capt Monticella Ky. E. A Street
Lieut 14th Ten Ripley Miss. R Vallant, Lieut Ark Batt. Hotsprings ark.
T. C. Bookter Capt Miss cavl. Starkaville Miss. The following number
of the above Brethren were then Baptized by Dr. Handy. Capt. W. F. Gorden
of Va Lieut F. H. McChristion, of Ark Lieut Jasper Horne, of Tenn. E. L.
Bell of Va. F. M. Noble, of Texas, John Paul of Va.
After the administration of the ordinance of baptism. the elements
representing the broken body and shed blood of our Lord and Savior.
Jesus Christ. were placed on the table and those who believed on his
name gathered around the board. Here was truly an interesting scene.

12

and one that Angels delighted to witness. The communicants were more than two hundred in number, and there not being seats for all, they arranged themselves promiscuously around the sacred board on the ground. The audience gathered around and in silence surveyed the scene The four ministers Dr Handy Capt Sanford Capt Harris and Lieut Thomas, stood one side the table and those just Baptized on the other. The bread was broken by our venerable Dr Handy. And was given to the discipl-es with that Solemn injunction brother "take eat this is my Body" and he took the cup and gave thanks and gave it to them saying "drink ye all of it. for this is my blood of the new testament which is shed for the rem-ission of sins. For as often as you eat this bread and drink this cup ye do shew the Lord's death till he come. Not a sound was heard save the low soft tread of those who bore the sacred elements to their brethren. A Hy-mn was sung and the impressive service was over, and that band of disciples seperated, never to meet again perhaps under simul-ar circumstances. They had met that day many of them for the first time and had drank of the same cup and mingled their voices in suppli-cation to a throne of grace. they parted, and when shall they all com-mune with their God together again. They had been thrown tog-ether and might soon be torn asunder never to meet again until gathered around the throne of Him who is to judge the quick and dead." Some had that day for the first time. Tasted the broken body and shed blood of their Saviour, and rejoiced in the hope of heaven. On the day following certificates of church membership were given to those who had been admitted to full fellowship on the day befor The desig

the certificates was the commendation of the Brethren to all christian churches when ever and wherever presented, and as a special recommendation to any particular church the brother might wish to connect himself with.

Appendix G

Tennessee Civil War Veteran's Questionnaire, completed by Lieutenant James Vance Walker

In 1914, the state of Tennessee, led by Dr. Gus Dyer, the Tennessee State Archivist, sought to record the memories of it's surviving Civil War veterans. A questionnaire developed by Dr. Dyer, was mailed to Confederate and Union veterans throughout the state. By 1922, 1,650 completed forms were returned. Among those returned was the questionnaire completed by James Vance Walker.

Below is the questionnaire with Walker's responses:

In case the space following any question is not sufficient for your answer, you may write your answer on a separate piece of paper. But when this is done, be sure to put the number of the question on the paper on which the answer is written, and number the paper on which you write your answer.

Read all the questions before you answer any of them. After answering the questions given, if you desire to make additional statements, I would be for you to add as much as you desire.

1. State your full name and present post office address:

    James V. Walker, Calhoun, Tenn.

2. State your age now:

    84 years old the 14th day of January last

3. In what State and county were you born?

    State of Tennessee Bradley County

4. Were you a Confederate or Federal soldier?

    Confederate

135

5. Name of your Company?

   G; 3rd Tenn. Inf. Vol.

6. What was the occupation of your father?

   Farmer

7. Give full name of your father: _____ born at _____;
   in the County   of _____; State of _____; He lived
   at _____; Give also any particulars concerning him, as
   official position, war services, etc.; books written by him, etc.:

   **William H. Walker; don't know; don't know; Tennessee; near
   Calhoun; he belonged to Co. G 3rd Regt. Tenn. Vol.**

8. Maiden name in full of your mother: _____; she was the
   daughter of: _____ (full name) _____and his wife
   _____   (full   name)   _____;   who   lived   at
   _____.

   Polly Poe; Balium Poe; don't know; don't know;

9. Remarks on ancestry. Give here any and all facts possible in
   reference to your parents, grandparents, great=grandparents,
   etc., not included in the foregoing as where they lived, offices
   held. Revolutionary or other war service; what country they
   came from to America; first settled – county and State. Always
   giving full names (if possible), and never referring to an
   ancestor simply as such without giving the name. It is desirable
   to include every fact possible, and to that end the full and exact
   record from old Bibles should be appended on separate sheets
   of this size, thus preserving the facts from loss.

   (No Answer)

10. If you owned land or other property at the opening of the war, state what kind of property you owned, and state the value of your property as near as you can:

none

11. Did you or your parents own slaves? If so, how many?

none

12. If your parents owned land, state about how many acres.

none

13. State as near as you can the value of all the property owned by your parents, including land, when the war opened.

(No Answer)

14. What kind of house did your parents occupy? State whether it was a log house or frame house or built of other material, and state the number of rooms it had:

My father was a renter owned no house of his own

15. As a boy and young many, state what kind of work you did. If you worked on a farm, state to what extent you plowed, worked with a hoe and did other kinds of similar work. (Certain historians claim that white men would not do work of this sort before the war.)

I plowed hoed sowed reaped cleard [sic] land etc. My father was a poor man raised a large family 6 boys and 4 girls I was the oldest and had to work.

16. State clearly what kind of work your father did, and what the duties of your mother were. State all the kinds of work done in the house as well as you can remember – that is, cooking, spinning, weaving, etc.:

(No Answer)

17. Did your parents keep any servants? If so, how many?

none

18. How was honest toil – as plowing, hauling and other sorts of honest work on this class – regarded in your community? Was such work considered respectable and honorable?

yes

19. Did the white men in your community generally engage in such work?

yes

20. To what extent were there white men in your community leading lives of idleness and having others do their work for them?

(No Answer)

21. Did the men who owned slaves mingle freely with those who did not own slaves, or did slaveholders in any way show by their actions that they felt themselves better than respectable, honorable men who did not own slaves?

No difference that I can remember

22. At the churches, at the schools, at public gathering in general, did slaveholders and non-slaveholders mingle on a footing of equality?

I never knew any difference

23. Was there a friendly feeling between slaveholders and non-slaveholders in your community, or were they antagonistic to each other?

Friendly

24. In a political contest, in which one candidate owned slaves and the other did not, did the fact that one candidate owned slaves help him any in winning the contest?

Not that I ever knew

25. Were the opportunities good in your community for a poor young man, honest and industrious, to save up enough to buy a small farm or go in business for himself?

Not very good

26. Were poor, honest, industrious young men, who were ambitious to make something of themselves, encouraged or discouraged by slaveholders?

I never knew of any discouragement

27. What kind or school or schools did you attend?

Free schools

28. About how long did you go to school altogether?

Don't remember

29. How far was it to the nearest school?

Don't remember

30. What school or schools were in operation in your neighborhood?

Free schools

31. Was the school in your community private or public?

Public I suppose

32. About how many months in the year did it run?

About 3 months

33. Did the boys and girls in your community attend school pretty regularly?

Tolerably

34. Was the teacher of the school you attended a man or woman?

man

35. In what year and month and at what place did you enlist in the service of the Confederacy or of the Federal Government?

The 3rd day of May 1861. I enlisted in the service of the Confederacy at Calhoun, Tenn.

36. After enlistment, where was your Company sent first?

The 7th day of May 1861 we were sent to Knoxville, Tenn.

37. How long after enlistment before your Company engaged in battle?

About 2 months and 18 days

38. What was the first battle you engaged in?

Battle of Manassa [sic] or Bull run in Va. Fought the 21 day of July 1861.

39. State in your own way your experience in the War from this time on to its close. State where you went after the first battle – what you did and what other battles you engaged in, how long hey lasted, what the results were; state how you lived in camp, how you were clothed, how you slept, what you had to eat, how you were exposed to cold, hunger and disease. If you were in the hospital or prison, state your experience there:

In the spring of 1862 we came back to Tenn. In the fall of 1862 we went with Gen. Brag [sic] into Ky had a battle at Peraville [sic], Ky. Don't remember the dame came back to Tenn. In the winter of 1862 went to Vicksburg, Miss. In May 1862 the Yankes [sic] crossed the river below…Vicksburg came in behind us about the 18th of May 1863. We had a battle called the big black or Champion hill fight. We retreated…back to our….fortifications in Vicksburg and was under fire 47 days and nights on the 4th day of July 1863 General Pemberton surrendered his army of Confederates to Gen. Grant we was payrolled [sic] about the 15 of July 1863 and came home.

40. When and where were you discharged?

Taken the oath at Fort Delaware June 17th 1865

41. Tell something of your trip home.

   (No Answer)

42. Give a sketch of your life since the close of the Civil War, stating what kind of business you have engaged in, where you have lived, your church relations, etc. If you have held any office or offices, state what it was. You may state here any other facts connected with your life and experience which has not been brought out by the question:

   Farming

43. What kind of work did you take up when you came back home?

   Since 1874 I have been in Milling business. We took a remant [sic] of our command to Atlanta, Ga. After we were exchanged [from Vicksburg]. I was sent...back to Tenn. to help get up those of our Co. that had failed to report. I was 1st Lt. of the Co. and was captured by Bush Whackers the 1st day of February 1864. Sent as a prisoner of war first to Camp Chase, Ohio. From there to Fort Delaware; arrived at Fort Delaware March the 27th 1864 held as a prisoner of war until June 17th 1865. Was released by taking the oath of alegiants [sic] to the United States. Sent home with free transportation to Knoxville, Tn. Arrived in Calhoun Tenn. June 23 day of 1865. Back to No. 43, as to my church relation, I joined the Methodist Church South the 23 day of August 1853. I very poorly served the Church as trustee class leader and Exarter (Exhorter).

44. On a separate sheet, give the names of some of the great men you have known or met in your time and tell some of the

142

circumstances of the meeting or incidents in their lives. Also add any further personal reminiscences (Use all of the space you want.)

(No Answer)

45. Give the names of all of the members of your Company you can remember (If you know where the Roster is to be had, please make special note of this.)

(No Answer)

46. Give the NAME and POST OFFICE ADDRESS of any living Veterans of the Civil War, whether members of your Company or not; whether Tennesseans or from other States.

J.K.P. Gidens, Capt; J.V. Walker, 1st Lt; Isaac Ledbetter, 2nd Lt.; J.C. ___man, 3rd Lt.; A.F. Rogers, 1st Sgt.; John K. Ball, 2nd Sgt.; S.H. Hacker, 3rd Sgt.; W.H. Pearce, 4th Sgt.; S.M. Morgan, 5th Sgt. J.K.P. Ball, 1st Corp.; J.S. Freeman, 2nd Corp.; E.C. Foster, 3rd Corp.; Privates: David Brock, B.G. Brock, S.S. Bishop, J.W. Bishop, Samuel Bramet, J.B. Bonner, John Carrol, W.E. Crowder, M.E. Calaway, W.N. Casey, Albert Coffman, J____ Dennis, T.H. Dill, W.B Erwin, J.R. Erwin, W.J. Farmer, John Goforth, W.N. Goforth, Thomas Gibbs, B.C. Giddens, T.H. Hamilton, J.W. Jenkins, Benjamin Kibble, Lewis Ledbetter, M.V. Ledbetter, Jackson Ledbetter, J.E. Ledbetter, G.F. Lemons, W.S. Morgan, J.A. Morgan, V. Mastiller, J.M. Martin, Jo B. McCarty, W.E. McMinn, E.W. Only, R.J. Only, Levi Only, B.F. Perkins, S.E.A. Rymer. I am the only one that is living [of] our co. that we know of.

Bibliography

Handy, Isaac, *United States Bonds or Duress by Federal Authority; A Journal of Current Events During Imprisonment of Fifteen Months at Fort Delaware [Baltimore, MD: Turnbull Brothers, 1874]*

Mary Guthrie, personal correspondence with the author

Don Handy, personal correspondence with the author

King James Bible

Fort Delaware Society, Delaware City, DE

Library of Congress, Washington DC

National Archives, Washington DC

Lloyd's Topographic Map of Georgia (1864)

Tennessee Civil War Veteran's Questionnaire, 1914, Tennessee State Archives, Nashville, TN

Laura Lee, Interpretive Program Manager & Park Historian, Fort Delaware State Park, personal correspondence with the author

Joe Walker is a native of Arkansas and a life-long civil war enthusiast. He is a founding member of the Friends of Jenkins' Ferry, (Arkansas Battlefield) as well as the Jenkins' Ferry Chapter of the Military Order of Stars and Bars. In addition, he was a founding member of the General James McPherson camp of the Sons of Union Veterans and is a member of the Seven Generals Camp of the Sons of Confederate Veterans. His family history is rich in Civil War history with ancestors serving in both the Union and Confederate armies. He and his family live in the Central Arkansas area.

For more information about the author, including opportunities for him to speak to your group or to attend a book signing, visit his website www.1864arkansas.com

Made in the
USA
Middletown, DE